Remarks On Existential Therapy: A Self Help Guide to Happiness

Jack R Ernest

Copyright

First Printing: June 2022

ISBN: 978-1-4716-7553-9

Introduction

'Perfection is Perception.'

An article in the newspaper caught my eye once. It discussed a method of measuring happiness among countries, which was in effect measuring the happiness of people. It achieved this feat through the Happy Planet Index (HPI) which measured wellbeing of an individual as opposed to wealth among other things. Initially I would have assumed that the western wealthy countries like the USA and those in west Europe would score the highest in this study. But I was wrong. The happiest countries in the world were actually the poorest. Places like Costa Rica, Vietnam and Belize all made the top five countries that inhabited the happiest of people.

So what has gone wrong with the capitalistic economies whose richness and GDP is mountain high? Let us compare the two extremes: Wealthy versus Poor. The poorer countries contained people who were all on par with each other. A lot of them lived in the countryside's and worked on farms. Many of these people were paid the same basic wage and could not gain wage increases. They also worked in areas wherein the work was extremely repetitive by nature: farm labourers and construction. It is an almost socialist dichotomy in which everyone is treated the same. Contrast this with the capitalist dominated western culture of sky scrapers and pavements awash with money. In this region people are competitive. They desire to be better than their co-worker. They can achieve more than their neighbour and henceforth set out to do so. They grow up not on farms but in environments where they receive more and more and thus carry this methodology of thinking into their adult lives. Their childhoods are dominated by being the most popular and they do not grow out of this mentality. Alas they put too much pressure on themselves to achieve unlike their poor counterparts and when these demands are not met, they become unhappy. The template for the ideal western man is marriage, family and work and he must live in accordance with these ideals. Now the man who meets these requirements does not need to fear; but the man who fails to exceed these expectations turns on himself and given the number of people in this world, very few people do meet what is covertly requested of them.

Perfection is perception. The poor are happy with their lives because happiness is to them working on a farm and tending to day to day farming activities. The western man is unhappy with who he is despite possessing a wealthier life than his third world friend. So one individual has no money and yet is content; the other individual is drenched with money and is unhappy. This is because happiness (the perfect life) is just a matter of perception. One person wakes up happy just to be alive; the other individual wakes up and tries to gain happiness through external gratification and there is a difference. One either wakes up happy with who there are or they do not. Treating happiness as something that can traded or earned or bought is not the correct way to deal life's cards. The method to navigate life's choppy straits is to just be happy with who you are regardless of your wealth, status or image. By doing this one cannot lose in life. If they achieve, they achieve. If they do not accomplish, they still have themselves. The perfect life is just ones interpretation of what is the perfect life. You are your own genius and your own executioner. You can be Michelangelo or Thomas de Torquemada. It depends on your perception. The former once said that every block of stone has a statue inside it. As such every man and woman alive can find happiness within themselves. They must chisel away the demons and be grateful for their existence. I have seen homeless men who are content to just sit by a bridge and collect pennies that are more jubilant in their lifestyle than some CEOs who must live with stress after stress. The perfect life depends on the individuals interpretation of what is the perfect life. There is no standard other than what we deem so to be the standard. Ones salvation lies in the frozen lake that is your heart. Melt it and set yourself free. The journey you take with your feet is nothing compared to the journey that takes place in your soul.

With this collection of notes I will attempt to portray this material rat race that has infested the minds of the western capitalist world and also suggest a change to the philosophy of living along the lines of the Existentialist/Buddhist strain of thought.

Chapter 1

The Mind

'A man is his unconscious mind.'

The unconscious mind dictates far more than we give it credit.

The reason why advertisement agencies earn fortunes is because of the unconscious mind and how it processes information mainly in the form of sight and hearing without the conscious awareness of the individual.

One will notice how a song if played repetitively on the radio suddenly becomes fixed in the mind of the individual, even though they may not know the name of the song or the artist behind it.

This is because the song has filtered into the unconscious mind over the course of days and the unconscious mind has become used to it.

How does one learn to type with speed? How does one put on their vehicle indicator at junctions? How does one respond to another in conversation? These are all done unconsciously with minimal conscious input.

The unconscious mind Freud said was the submerged part of the iceberg whereas the conscious mind was the tip.

The unconscious mind governs emotion in a conversation or when watching a film. The eyes and ears receive stimulus which influence the unconscious mind and it responds with chemicals being produced which alter your feeling.

It is so powerful and it is manipulated daily by adverts, sales representatives and politicians.

The reason I touch on this subject is that there is one other serious element to the unconscious mind which rarely goes noticed and this is conformity.

As a child you were indoctrinated with socialization and conversation from a very young age. This then endeavours to make one more sociable as they grow older.

It also means that conversation becomes the fodder of the intellect because just like the body needs water to survive, the mind needs conversation to cultivate itself.

Because of conversation and education, we are implored to live life a certain way. However, because of this shadow that is cast, we live in unconscious fear.

One should never be desperate to live because to be so is to live in fear. The two are linked to each other. We are afraid of others opinions so we become desperate to appease them covertly. In our desperation to win their endorsement we fall further into the snake pit of anxiety. Each man and woman sees their own parents and is put under pressure to continue the cycle of families. They then look at their friends and see them all settling down with families of their own and fear being left stranded. The problem is that it is difficult to escape this menace for we are from childhood addicted to conversation. In our want to converse we are put under stress unconsciously to conform to the principles of the herd.

People say life is stressful. Life is not stressful but rather it is the people in your life that make it stressful. It is friends, family and peers that make one's life pressurised.

Hence people grow up in such a manner that they partake with others, they enjoy liaising with others and they use others as a drug akin to a drug addict who uses heroin to make him feel better.

The universal man uses conversation to stimulate his mind. Conversation is the majority's addiction. When one chats or meets friends, chemicals are discharged in the corners of the brain and help such a person feel better.

Chemicals in the brain determine our mood. There are only two types of people in this world: Addicts and those who are addicted to their own existence. People think in terms of thoughts and not chemicals. It never dawns on them that the reason they are unhappy is rooted in thought and chemicals.

Conversation is thus the drug that the common people use. This is why socialization is so rampant in today's society. It comes from youth because when you were young you were subjected to socialization at a young age and thus the mind adapts to demand an incessant supply of language to keep itself happy.

Socialization from a young age is vital for the world because this serves to make us conform indiscriminately in that we don't realize we are doing so. So because of language and that we enjoy meeting others, we behave in an all too predictable fashion.

Consequently, we do too much talking and not enough thinking. This socialization at a young age is vital to become fully human, but it also serves to make us the equivalent of everyone else.

The disciplines of psychology and economics would not exist if we were all distinct. That we behave in an all too absolute fashion is the result of this unconscious drive to behave in the way in which one does.

But everyone behaves the same however and thus everyone's unconscious mind is thinking in the same way.

The unconscious mind is deciding what you as an individual want in life. It commands your desires. If you buy a certain product in a shop you can rest assured that the unconscious mind had a say in picking that particular product. We are condemned to choose.

Men are unconsciously programmed to want sex. Women are unconsciously programmed to want to raise a family.

We develop habits due to training of the unconscious mind. When you talk to someone you may do something peculiar which is done on instinct. When you play sports, you rely on pure instinct as you do when you drive.

We are lied to daily by the powers that be who proclaim we are in charge consciously of our destiny. Very few people are that knowledgeable I must attest. Most people live on instinct.

Conversation and enjoyment rely on this instinct to be laudable. For example, take a conversation with a friend for that matter. You say something to which the friend responds on instinct, to which you respond on instinct and so the conversation flows. You are not given five minutes to think up a reply. No, one must respond on the spot.

This is why facial interviews are so important. We all look good in the CV, but do we sound good? How one speaks is indicative of how they think. Those who speak well have been properly socialized and will think in a form similar to 99% of the world. Employers are thus looking not for people who can critically think, but rather people who can't think.

They are looking for people who spend far too much time captivated in the various facets of life that they dare not examine why they live.

Critical thinkers are dangerous to businesses because they do not buy into the pseudo-prostitution that is daily existence.

The cynic knows that he is selling himself whereas the common individual sees work as something that must be done because that is how the world turns on its axis.

People only see the blue skies. They cannot see the universe. They cannot see that they are vaulting across space at a lightening quick speed. They cannot see the sun even when they stare at it.

Life thus becomes the nine to five, five day working week and enjoyment at the weekend. Now why can't people see this? They are existentially blind because they are programmed from childhood socialization not to see and the world although round becomes about politics, economic growth and materialistic in nature.

Language is why we are human, yet it is also why one fails to perceive. We place too much emphasis on acceptable communication skills and appeasing the will of others that we repudiate the realities of the universe.

It is because of this unconscious decision making process, which is beyond the control of the average individual that the men and women of this world conform. They do so without conscious thought.

One thinks they are working or marrying because that is what they themselves wish to do.

Unfortunately, this is true for the vast majority people. They walk because everyone else does. They talk because everyone else does. They live thus because everyone else does. This living is unconscious. One sees how everyone else lives and mimics it unconsciously.

Boredom

'In life you must choose between boredom and everything else.'

Buddhism lectures its followers on many things. It tells us to forego the materialistic side of things in favour of the simple life. It tells us to stop hunting happiness and instead to just be happy.

One other thing that it strives to teach is that man must become tolerant of his boredom to become free. Our lives are a constant battle against boredom.

Man lives to evade boredom and thus is a slave to avoiding it. We go out and meet people, we watch a film and we read a book or listen to the news to negate boredom. All man's problems arise from his inability to sit quietly by himself and tolerate his existence. So, a man feels bored and then does something that he may regret to neutralize that boredom.

All our struggles can be rewound back towards the quest to avoid boredom. If we could just be cheerful with ourselves and more accepting of ourselves we would live a richer life bereft of pain.

But no, we become servants to addictions because we seek to avoid boredom. It is said that man is the only animal that cannot tolerate himself. Man, unlike a dog cannot sit and remain passive for hours at a time. He must be entertained. He must be passing the time with some activity.

The pursuit of happiness becomes an addiction. People say when they have achieved X, Y and Z they will be happy.

But like all addictions it is only provisional and the mind reboots itself and demands more.

There is happiness one hunts which is an addiction and there is happiness one possesses which is freedom from addiction.

We escape one addiction to another. We leap from one tyranny to another. We are indoctrinated to not be self-aware. We are conditioned to escape unto others.

We are martyrs to our own incapacity to enjoy ourselves. We must lose ourselves in the world in order to pass the time. But this sometimes means we go too far and we make mistakes. We stare into the abyss for too long and eventually we fall in. All life's problems arise from our poor tolerance of boredom.

We are addicted to feeling good. We want others to make us feel good. It's a game. We say to ourselves we won't value that other person unless they emotionally subsidize us. The problem is we become inured on other folks to make us feel comforted and reject our own existence. Education when young has us drip fed on others. So much that we cannot tolerate our own naked self.

If you can indulge your boredom then you will become free. If you can sit by yourself and be content, then you will become free. If you can gaze and gaze into the stars at night and find solace in such an activity you will become free.

A relationship and a film are both means to escape. We pour ourselves into them to escape boredom. But they are dangerous because what happens if they fail to assist someone escape. To escape oneself is to tolerate one's boredom and is the best means of escape. People need to learn to be happy to just be.

Become more self-aware of what you are doing and why you do it. The common man is no different from the drug addict whose life is centred on heroin, except the common man's addictions are conversation and entertainment.

Time is so precious and yet we are pressed to kill it at every given moment. We are compelled to do so because we cannot handle the boredom. To become free, one must revel in their ennui. They must become accepting of life. They must find warmth in the frigid monotony.

We are schooled to look for happiness or to look for love but they can only be found deep within. Our salvation lies within us, not around us. We are emotionally dependent on external aspects for our happiness and when one stakes their joy on others they most certainly play with dice.

Identity

'Man is his identity.'

Our identity along with our socio-economic status leads us to evolve an egocentric view of our lives.

Our identity is our name, face and personality.

Because we have a unique identity we think that we have an anomalous status in the world.

We thus traverse through life under the illusion that we are distinct.

We live as if we are a god and immortal.

As long as we are popular our identity is positive.

So as long as we are in demand in life, we remain warm.

But what becomes of old age when we lose our looks and possibly our ability. We never realize our own worthlessness, our own repetition and our own mortality until it is too late.

People are deluded when they are sane. They put an over emphasis on their identity and develop a narcissistic view of their existence. They feel they are worthy.

Their identity leads them to believe that they have greater merit in the world than they should.

When they should see atoms of tissue they see a face.

When they should see letters of a word they see a name.

When they should see neurons firing on synapses they see a personality.

Our unconscious awareness of our identity (name, face and personality) coupled with the fact that we can talk using language, strives to make man believe he is distinguished.

He comes to regard himself as a god over all other animals.

He thus comes to believe that he deserves more in life if he is under achieving.

He fails to see that he exists on a planet that is spherical. Daily life is flat and about popularity and family and work.

Identity is so important to the world economically for it means man turns a blind eye on the darkness of the universe in favour of this shallow existence we call life.

His identity urges him to conform and hides the existential truth from him.

As long as man has an inflated view of his existence through his identity he will not be free.

Freedom comes from realizing the awful truths of existence. Freedom comes from the anxiety of life. Be addicted only to your own freedom. We wait for our world to change us, when only we can change our world. One must give birth to themselves daily.

Perception
'Life is how you perceive it.'

There is no bad weather in life just a poor perception. If you keep waiting for the rain to stop, you will never live.

One does not need to modify their life to advance their life. What they need to do is revise their perception. If you adjust your perception towards life, you will reform your life regardless.

How one perceives life stems from the etiquette of the prison they grew up in.

So instead of chasing life, just accept life. Instead of being in pursuit of the good life, be happy with your life.

Love your existence, every atom of it. The love that one can receive is nothing in comparison to the love they can give to themselves.

Imagine one is in a race. One's life prior to examination of these notes has been about the finale. By coming first at the finish line, you reap the rewards. My philosophy makes the order of the finish irrelevant. It is about enjoying the race regardless of the finish and when you enjoy the journey you will enjoy the accomplishment.

Changing one's life does not involve a complete transformation of one's life image wise. This is what capitalism has led you to believe. That in order to be happy you must be doing: A, B and C.

To enhance your life one just needs to reshape their perception of what is the good life.

The good life is just existing. It is not about being popular or working the highly paid job or marrying the ideal person.

The perfect life is simply just being alive. Become embroiled in your despair, for a life without some trauma is no life at all.

People don't realize how lucky they are to be alive.

They are lucky that they live on this planet, that it is full of water and in the right position in space to enable liquid water.

People never realize how finely tuned the universe is to support life.

People don't realize how lucky they are to be able to realize they are alive.

Textbook life is about work and relationships and they block the actual realities of existence. This is the result of narcissism, be it basic or full blown.

People get up at seven and go to work and completely refute the greater universe.

Life becomes about the 9 to 5 race and when they fail at this aspect of life they become depressed.

We need to become more aware of how insignificant we are and from this we can perhaps escape the commoditized world of professional and relationship gain.

People are so committed in life that they are indifferent to the existential realities. They only see the blue skies and other people.

They don't see the size of the universe. They turn a blind eye on evolution.

If you realize the existential facts of life you may just enjoy life more rather than worrying.

To change yourself you need not change your life, just change your perception.

Life is beautiful, it is painful; it is simple, it is hard; it is everything, it is nothing. It all depends on your interpretation. How one sees life is a matter of interpretation. It can be great or bad, it just depends on one's perception.

A man is both the thunder and the darkness of his existence. His own perception is what determines him.

Marketing is so powerful. You go into a restaurant and look at the menu and you see all these exquisite meals that you could eat. But the restaurant through marketing hypes up the meals just so you will buy them. Likewise, the dream life is hyped up so you will conform. You get told that by doing X, Y and Z, you will become happy.

A man is imprisoned by his own walls of perception and if he alters his perception those walls will crumble.

Following

'Man is compelled to follow.'

There are very few individuals in society. We are all similar. We follow what the majority demands and we do it unconsciously. We crawl on the shadows of the crowd.

In order to feel alive, we must affix ourselves to certain sects. Often we follow not because we are free to do so, but because of fear and boredom.

Thus, people support a sports team or become devoted fans of a famous person.

They follow these organizations or individuals because they strive to feel alive. They strive to feel alive so that they can nullify the stress of boredom. They live to be gratified, which is narcissism, which is unhealthy. We define our substance and our meaning on endorsement from society and as such we prostitute ourselves daily to appease its convictions.

But people don't realize they are following. They don't realize they are living the same life as everyone else.

Nothing is ever achieved by doing what everyone else does. To earn you must do what no one else does. You must create what hasn't been created; solve what hasn't been solved; live a life that hasn't been lived.

But the will to follow is engrained us all from childhood. We like to be part of the herd. We dislike individuality. We covertly praise those who conform. We don't value our own solitude. The proof is in how we pour ourselves into others to live.

The system is self-perpetuating. Conformity begets conformity. The herd respects those who submit to what the herd demands. It is borne out of a sublime fear of opinions and not by conscious choice. We conform ultimately because we are afraid of being socially castrated by the majority.

The person you love, the film you adore, the club you devote your life to is all irrelevant. Billions of people love, billions of people adore and billions of people devote.

In effect through one's unconscious desire to follow, they follow the template of conformity. They conform not because they consciously wish to, but because they unconsciously are piloted to do so.

The masses of men are no different from the spring lambs that are led to the slaughter except the slaughterhouse is what we call everyday life.

Capitalism will thus endure not just because of greed but because its pawns are so obligated to follow. It will endure because we infect the individual with narcissism, which makes them obsess over the material life.

We live the life of many. We are nothing special. Following ushers us to believe that we are inimitable. We say unconsciously we have an incomparable partner and a distinct soul, when we are just fodder for the 1% who really gain in life. The 1% laugh all the way to the bank.

If one becomes acquainted of why they choose, they then can negotiate their own lives better. If one can see what they are doing, they can rectify what they are doing. Jung said that those who look inwards awaken. Those who are able to observe themselves can discern themselves better.

We are unconsciously persuaded to believe that we are exceptional because following permits us to believe we are exceptional. The lover, the sports team, the television all excite us and make us feel alive and in feeling alive we put to sleep the harsh realities of the universe.

The greatest trick the economic system plays is convincing you it is not a system. It becomes in the eyes of this immature individual "life." Society cannot see that they are brainwashed because this brainwashing is called life.

What invariably happens is we wake up when we are sixty and look at a shadow in the mirror and realize we wasted the best part of our lives chasing a better one.

Youth is wasted on the young. We are so engaged in this petty shallow existence of material yield that we let our greatest asset waste.

Don't follow the crowd because you are afraid. Follow your own heart and soul to the bitter end. We spend our whole lives trying to find that other person that we fail to find ourselves.

Don't follow the crowd unless you are prepared to settle for being nothing.

Wisdom must be self-learned. There is no tapestry on how to live; man, himself must discover it.

Conformism

'In conforming we betray our very existence.'

Why do we all live identical lives? Why do we all wish to get married? Why do we all work? Why are we lectured on the value of relationships? Why are good communication skills demanded?

The answer to all these questions is one word: Conformity. Conformity is the fanaticism of the majority. We are radicalized on conformity. We are the soldiers of conformism. We inhabit the theatre of conformists.

Why do women have long hair and men short hair? That is conformism.

Conformity is the unconscious drive to behave like the masses do. We are products of our environment and environment stipulates that we should behave certain ways. Your environment should be a product of you; you should not be a product of your environment.

There are two people inside everyone: The man who wears a mask and the man when he removes that mask; the man in the midst of others and the man in solitude when he can be himself; the man who lives under pretences and the man himself.

The neuro-typical possesses an unnatural fear of solitude. Through education and family and friends plus the incapacity to tolerate boredom, people seek out others and condemn the loneliness and perhaps themselves to the gallows.

It must be understood that the drive to conform is unconscious. One conforms because they are unconsciously implored to do so.

From a very young age we are taught that the prototype for our lives is work and relationships. But these are not necessarily the correct ways in which to live. They are ways to live, but not by any means the only way to live.

We want to be wanted. Being wanted makes us feel good and hence why we approach life in such a conformist method. The man must be successful and the woman must be good looking because both these qualities increase our desirability and make us feel wanted which in turn makes us feel content.

Yet we feel compelled to live in a certain way that mimics the behaviour of our friends and family and we are not happy until they are happy. People waste their lives and fall into unhappiness over their failure to be normal.

It is not just coincidental that men and women who grew up with working parents tend to follow their parents into work and those who grew up in poverty tend to remain in poverty. The reason is because they unconsciously impersonate the behaviour of their parents.

They observe how their parents live and seek to replicate that behaviour. It is unconscious conformity without realizing it. People automatically assume to uphold the law. Apply this logic to everyday life.

We spend so much time living that we do not realize we are alive.

We are so intrigued by life that we cannot see ourselves.

We live on instinct so much that we refuse to rationally think.

Why do men have predominantly short hair and women long hair? Why do we swarm to be in a relationship? Why do we work till we retire?

One reason why people conform is because there often is no other choice. It is either: Conform, non-conform or become a criminal.

One must become more self-aware as to why they are doing what they do. Why do we live in accordance with everyone else? One does so because they are under pressure to conform.

It is friends and family that dictate how one should live. They are the ones who put people under burden to live a certain way and achieve in a certain way. We are under so much invisible pressure from family, friends and peers to succeed in life. They are the ones who aim the rifle at our forehead.

Get off social media. Social media does two things: A) That we are exposing ourselves to society means we must try and accrue a positive label from society. So, we must expend time, energy and possibly money in fabricating this façade so that the viewing public will approve or be impressed by us. This creates anxiety. It is a form of suffering. B) You instinctively start comparing yourself to others, which only enhances anxiety.

The urge to conform is like the avoidance of anxiety. Men and women are striving to appease its will out of fear of being negatively labelled by friends and family. It is not the fists of man that we fear but his eyes. If the whole world were blind, we would have a much simpler existence. The camera has always existed in the form of retinas.

One is not free. One is living on the will of conformity. You date because everyone else does it and this is what is demanded silently. You work because everyone else does it and this is what is demanded silently. You live the textbook life because a textbook life is how everyone lives and this is what is demanded silently.

People see themselves through others perception. The goal is to see yourself through yourself and not others.

The system makes people unhappy and then the system says, if you do X, Y and Z you can become happy and so many believe it. A young woman who deems herself unattractive then spends a fortune in plastic surgery in order to become happy.

Overcoming your urge to have the branded clothes is what you need to do to be happy. You need to apply this solution to your whole life. You need to overcome your narcissism. Of course, the economic system does not want you to do this. The economic system wants you to be narcissistic. It is narcissism that makes you buy a pair of jeans worth a hundred dollars instead of one worth ten dollars.

Man is in chains and the chains are conformity. He lives according to the script of conformity.

We live in anguish of a negative opinion and this implores us to conform.

Opinion dictates the world. Man is guided by its wind. We live so as not to let our friends and family cast a desolate judgement on us.

Unfortunately, when we do not reach the standards of what is covertly demanded, we become depressed.

We are in a bind psychologically. We want to live our own lives and yet we must conciliate to the will of others.

This creates anxiety. A lot of our anxiety is over our inability to succeed in accordance with the script that is written for us.

They need people to conform; they need people to marry and have children. How do they encourage or promote this? They frame it, as the behavioural economists might say, that conforming is romantic and idyllic. Falling in love and having children becomes this one thing you have to experience as a human being. People then become so afraid of missing out on this dream life, that they conform on instinct.

To overcome this one must realize that they are not free. The first step of becoming free is in accepting that you are not free. One must see that they are just conforming to the will of others. Through being self-aware of this they can then accurately plot their course within life.

We are all identical despite our names and faces. We all live the same infertile lives of repetition.

The reason the world conforms is largely due to the institutionalization of language from an early age. Language makes man conform. It makes him the same as everyone else. We abuse our existence through conforming.

Solitude I feel is a great friend with regards to finding oneself during turmoil. People need to spend a little less time around others and more time around themselves. Discovery can only come from within and the greatest thing one will discover in life is themselves.

Statisticians

'We are all statisticians.'

Who do we accept? Who do we reject? Who do we ignore?

We are preoccupied with a popularity contest. We play an unconscious variation of game theory with everyone we encounter in life.

We are all making inferences about who we meet and they make inferences about us.

---That person looks nice.

---That person would improve my image.

---That person is sub-standard.

We are all statisticians. We all make judgments about who we encounter. We all convey basic narcissistic traits.

We are so obsessed with how others live that we end up not living ourselves.

We are so absorbed in the lives of others that our own life slips by.

---That person has more than I.

---That person has a better image.

---That person has greater attributes.

We play the Cold War with everyone we meet.

We are all judging and making inferences about the people we encounter. We are so fascinated in the life of the many, that we mimic the life of the many.

Just as we assess others, we also assess ourselves and try to minimize negative comments about ourselves. This is narcissism.

This is why we are captivated by our own image and demand that it be golden. We want to appease the unconscious will of others. Making others happy makes us happy and that is our mistake.

Man is addicted to conformity and this addiction is unconscious. Man lives but does not realize why he lives. Just as an animal responds to urges, man too responds to the world he sees around him. Conformity is the illusion and just as we are fooled by the magician, we are fooled by life.

The capitalist ethos has made us greedy. It has made us fanatical with image and with others and how they judge.

Happiness lies in first realizing that you are involved in this game and secondly by rejecting this game in favour of your own personal freedom. In order to become happy, you must mature. You must become grateful.

Your freedom lies in being yourself and accepting yourself for what you are. Ones liberation is found in gratitude.

All our anxieties lie in the eyes of others. Every troubling thought one feels for the world is connected to people in some way or form. This is why solitude is so favourable because it alleviates the people from the equation and lets man find some peace. It is a peace that comes dropping slow and that one finds in their delicate heart.

Our anxieties lie in the eyes of others as do our aspirations. Why do we want success? We do so, because success makes us look good in front of our peers. Education has us in a psychological bind in that we live to appease our friends and family at the expense of realizing our inner self.

Education is the opium of the masses. It has people doped on society values. People consequently lose esteem over their failure to achieve mediocrity. The fatal mistake we make is that we measure our esteem in being desired. Education is an ideology like communism that enslaves its participants. There are people caged by concrete walls that are more liberated than the conventional man.

The sad thing is that people's lives are scripted and marriage is the theme of that script. Ask a group of adolescents what they want from life, most will say marriage. They have been polluted with it. Life is a stage play with an overused plot. They work, they date and they succeed.

It is better to become lost in search of yourself than to never find yourself at all, for the uncertainty and perhaps the pain is but a small price to pay for the privilege of discovering yourself. One has to find their niche in life. What is it that they are good at and more pertinent what is it that they enjoy being good at? It may be taken from the script of conformity, but then again it may not.

Psychological Mortgage
'It is friends and family that enslave us.'

We are used to the hearing about the bind that a financial mortgage places us in.

By taking out a mortgage we pretty much sell our future.

It ties us down to a job and conformity on the whole.

But there is also a psychological bind (mortgage) that shackles our mental freedom. This bind is induced not by the people you dislike but by the very people you turn to for support.

One of the big problems with being born into the family nucleus is the unconscious drive that we must too do the same. That we grew up as children with parents, strives to enforce this expectation that we will become parents ourselves.

Friends and family may support us but they also cripple our conscience with regards our freedom.

Friends and family put us in a psychological mortgage. They are the ones who hold us hostage. They are the ones we try to appease.

A lot of people are under the duress of what their friends and family covertly demand of them. What we crave in life is people; what we fear in life is their labels. It is a catch-22. On one side we need company to be of substance; on the other side company carries the threat of a negative opinion.

The mandate is silent. To impress your friends, you must ascribe to a certain way of life. To make your family content you must also live a certain way.

We stake our happiness on the lives of others and when we do so, we play with dice. All life's problems stem from others. If we feel shame, guilt or insignificant, it is usually connected to another person. We fear their labels and we are held in their vice grips. The solution is simple: Solitude. No man equals no problem. To be known in this world is the dilemma.

Friends and family unconsciously manipulate how you actually live. They quietly command that you attain certain things in life. They give birth to narcissistic traits that make you unhappy.

Very often we are led to marry and to work not because we truly wish to do these things but because our peers (friends and family) have latently told us to do so.

We wish to appease them and portraying a positive image in the mould of conformity is how we do this.

Parents want us to marry. This may never be explicitly stated but it is expected and hence we marry because of this unconscious bind.

Parents also want us to work in certain jobs. Again, it may never be explicitly stated but it is generally an expectation that the child will follow unconditionally. It is poison to stake ones future on others.

People unconsciously compare themselves to others. A person looks at what his or her friends have and demands the same of themselves. When the demands are not met, they fall into a depression. The very people who support us are often the ones who castigate our conscience

The whole concept of narcissism is that happiness is derived from impressing people. The diseased man says, "if I dress in that expensive suit, then people will be impressed by me." Likewise, the corrupted woman says, "if I am seen with that man, then people will be impressed." It is a herd-driven gratification. It is making people like you in order to like yourself. It makes one gratified, but it does not bring long term happiness. Like a shark that must move forward, the individual must keep succeeding, must keep impressing people, in order to stay alive. They suffer to be "happy" and tragically never become happy.

We are not really free or plotting our own course. The course is set by the winds of judgement of those closest to us. There is nothing that one can do for you that you cannot do for yourself.

People use endorsement to determine their happiness as in being wanted gives them emotional satisfaction. They are addicted to acclaim.

People thus live impoverished lives of repetition wherein they sail towards shores that have already been discovered rather than in search of the new lands. Conformity is a strait that is clichéd. By giving in unconsciously to the will of others we set fire to any freedom we possess. We are our own arsonists of despair. We are not free. We are in a psychological mortgage governed by the eyes of our dearest. We live how they want us to live and not how we wish to live.

Socialization teaches us that we cannot survive by ourselves. It teaches us that the company of others is required for the good life. If you can survive by yourself, you can survive any extreme. Learn to tolerate your own solitude and you will achieve in life. We have become so dependent on each other that solitude has become a nightmare.

We stake our future and its happiness on others. We say: When I have achieved this and that in life, I will be happy. But we are only chasing the labels of happiness and not happiness itself, for we attest that when we fall under such and such label, we can then declare our happiness. Our happiness is thus commoditized. It is dependent on certain parameters being obtained. We say we can't be happy until we are married or working.

The amount of people who let the seconds dissipate waiting for a better life. There is no other life. This is the only existence one has. Accept yourself, your flaws and your demons, before it is too damn late.

We are always in a state of dying: Dying to get older, dying to get rich, dying to marry, dying to live, dying to be happy and ultimately actually dying. As the saying goes, we live as if we will never die and die having never really lived. In our lust to live the good life we betray ourselves.

Idealism
'We want the good life.'

From a very young age we come to consent to what is demanded of us as we age.

We get indoctrinated with the ideals of life of which we must adhere to.

So much in fact that we become idealistic dreamers who refuse to accept reality.

How many people dream of their life further down the road?

---When I'm thirty I will be married.

---When I am married I will be happy.

---When I am earning money, I will be content.

Their lives are consumed escaping to the future and a stubborn refusal to live in the present.

They live their lives with the promise of reward at the destination and overlook the journey.

Our lives become narcissistically commoditized. We unconsciously learn that material achievement is the path to living the good life. Life is far too great to waste it on ideals.

In doing so we reject our naked selves as acceptable. We turn our very existence into failure that can only be alleviated by accomplishment. We put the fate of our happiness in others. It is almost as if we are too afraid to live by our own conviction.

Life thus becomes about the end and not the journey. The end is the ideal methodology of living based on conformism. We internally say that marriage, work and family are the stepping stones to happiness. We dismiss our own existence as a means to be happy and thus in this chase of happiness we remain unhappy.

Some of course achieve happiness through materialistic means but it is a hazardous happiness for what becomes of the individual when he or she no longer can achieve?

Very often these individuals use their children's lives as a prop to further their achievement. If the child achieves, the parent feels happy. But if the child fails the parent too fails.

We are doped on this idealism of "the good life." It is like a rainbow of which gladness lies at its end. But we keep chasing and chasing and never ever reach the end of the rainbow and die having forgotten to live.

We don't even chase happiness it must be asserted. We chase the labels that we assume will make us happy. Thus, a man says: When I have the pretty wife, the big house and the inflated financial account, then I will be happy. And the woman says: When I have the in-demand husband, the esteemed job and the family nucleus, I too will be happy. Their happiness is commoditized. It is based on labels that they advertise to their peers. When they win their contemporaries acclaim they thus feel content. Alas it is a diseased happiness that needs servicing just like any addiction and more to the point it is a happiness that will not survive the senility. The means to be happy as I have referenced throughout these notes is to just be happy to exist in this tense unforgiving universe.

Seeking approbation is the devil of our soul.

What makes people adhere to the rules of the road? A lot of it is unconscious. Seldom does someone defy the rules and drive erratically because they unconsciously are programmed not to do so.

Just be happy to exist. Be a realist. Life is tough. The universe is indifferent. But find consolation in your lonely existence and try to just be happy to be.

Change your perception of what is the ideal life. It is not work and family. The ideal life is simply being alive, so make the most of it.

The good life is more than a label. It is a feeling. There is "in love" the label and "in love" the feeling.

Life is but a flicker of light between birth and death and like thunder it disappears so abruptly.

If one tries to force the issue in life they will fail. If one tries to find friends, love or happiness, they will fail. These things originate from instinctive spontaneity. One cannot consciously try to have a friend. They are friends. One cannot consciously try to be in love, they simply love. One cannot consciously try to be happy. They either are happy or they are not. Paradoxically one can only find success, love or themselves when they are not looking. We spend our lives looking for success when existing is the only success. People search and search and are left searching at the end of it all. They search externally and fail to search within themselves.

Happiness is not the meaning of life. To love your life is the meaning and from this dichotomy happiness becomes collateral. One cannot try to be happy. No such thing exists. Try to be grateful to be alive and the happiness will pour from the skies. One must overcome their narcissistic gratification. One should attach their happiness to their own existence and not to another person or object.

We are unconsciously trained to only see happiness in relationships and careers. We are doped through education alike to believe that our success lies in them two facets of life. These are only models of happiness and not final by any means. If one is unconsciously trained to see existence on these two terms they can be trained to see happiness on other terms.

You cannot be happy with narcissism even if you possess minute quantities of it. It is a disorder of fear and threats. "If I do not do this, people will laugh at me. If I don't marry people will laugh at me. If I don't look attractive, people will laugh at me. If I don't work a certain job, people will laugh at me." Narcissists are to cut to the core of it afraid and that is why they conform, to retrieve admiration, which provides snippets of gratification, but it is a diseased and temporary happiness. Narcissists in order to mature must distance themselves from the herd, which is exceedingly difficult in this world.

Envy
'Envy is a subtle flattery.'

We impulsively compare and contrast ourselves with others. We are programmed to so from the capitalist ethos.

Those who fare poorly we do not fear and hence we feel nothing but ignorance for them.

But those who are our equal or perhaps better than us we feel contempt for.

Capitalism teaches us that we must be number one in order to be fulfilled. Capitalism teaches that happiness can be earned if people conform. So, if a person gets married and works they will procure the elusive happiness. Capitalism teaches that we are at the behest of others for our happiness. It is wrong. If you have to pay for your happiness you are doing it wrong.

The problem is not that we have too little but rather we have too much and do not appreciate what we have. Capitalism makes us want more and the man who is in want of much acquires very little.

It teaches that we have to be the most desirable if we want to be happy and hence why we expend so much energy in trying to be desirable.

It twists our mentality so much that we become envious of those who are deemed more desirable than ourselves. We become narcissistic.

The man may see another man who is more attractive looking, has more money or has a more attractive partner and feel envious.

The woman may look upon another woman in the same vein.

But their envy is just a façade for their positive estimation of these people. These other people possess things that are greater than what the envious person possesses. Their envy is just a form of flattery.

It says a lot about our current happiness when we feel envious of those who are jubilant. That is how greedy we are. We crave to be better than everyone else. We desire to be more successful and thus we calculate happiness in terms of material gain.

Envy corrupts so many in the capitalist world and many lives are wasted in being envious.

Capitalism wants envious patrons because they will go out and try to be better than those they are jealous of. It is a by-product of the capitalist dogma.

People don't want others to be happy living their own life. People want others to be the same mediocre person that most people are. They want them to conform because it means they are identical to each other.

One should never be envious of another because they will channel their youth into such jealously of themselves and the other. Many a man has thrown his life away because of his envy. He has wasted his early years in trying to be better than his competitor. We are all terrorists of a spent existence.

People are made insecure by virtue of the fact that they expose themselves to the herd.

If one is content enough to exist they will not be envious. If one is just happy to be, they will not fear the other individual.

Don't become involved in the race that is capitalism. You will waste your life in spite of another and it isn't worth wasting. You are invaluable as a person not because of your worth or your smile but rather because you simply are.

No intelligent mature individual ever feels envious of another person.

Concentrate on your own existence first and foremost. You must make yourself happy before you can make others happy.

But we are almost too afraid to just be happy as individuals. We are too afraid to just be. It is as if happiness must be warranted and is dependent on external gain.

One will never be happy so long as they objectify their happiness. If one quantifies their happiness on external objects, they play with dice.

Unconscious Training
'Change starts with the unconscious mind.'

To improve you must train your unconscious mind to behave differently. Conscious change is not enough. You are your instinct and to change you must circumvent your instinct. The problem is not that we refuse to learn but rather that we must unlearn what we have learned.

One must train their unconscious to just be happy to exist. One must reprogram their synapses to be grateful to wake up every morning.

This begins with conscious awareness of your unconscious response. Become consciously aware of how you instinctively react to what life demands of you.

Observe how you behave. Try to see the pattern.

Analyse the way you respond to questions, how you react to events and how you emotionally think.

Instinct mainly comprises of three elements:

---Conversation

If you want to change how you talk you must observe how you talk and then practise on what you wish to improve.

---Emotion

To change how you emotionally become involved in the qualities of life you must first realize what you are doing. When you read the paper or watch a sports match, you become emotionally involved. The same happens when you become involved with someone you like.

As you engage in these facets of life, your brain is releasing chemicals which make you enjoy the occasion.

If you realize this you can then determine your emotional response and realize that you are being emotional.

---Action

When you drive the car you drive on instinct. Observing how you behave in life and the realization that you act on instinct in response to life means you can then change how you react.

If you comprehend how you react you can influence how you react.

What it takes to modify your unconscious mind is the ability to observe yourself in another's eyes.

If you can visualize yourself as you live you can then tell yourself to change how you live.

But it takes time. You are trying to change your unconscious instinct into a more favourable response.

So instead of pursuing material gain in the form of relationships and work, you come to realize what you are doing and train your unconscious to no longer instinctively want them.

Through training your unconscious instinct you become existentially free and more in command of your life.

What is needed is less gratuitous talking and more critical thinking.

We are so desperate to live that we end up living unhappily. The individual that is desperate to enjoy themselves rarely does. People are so preoccupied with seeking endorsement from others that they stubbornly refuse to just accept their own naked self.

We seek friends not for their enthusiasm but for their endorsement.

The 21st century man and woman are under pressure. They are lost in an awesome wave being pulled in all directions. Society says marry and achieve or you will not be respected. As such they remain torn and lost in the ocean of gratification and they never find their island of gratitude.

Positive Thinking
'Think happiness, be happy.'

The capitalist ethos is as much a state of thinking as it is an ideology.

It poisons your thought into behaving in certain ways.

We are schooled on how happiness is to be earned and how life is to be bought.

One of the problems with capitalism is that it soils our thinking. We are told that we cannot be happy until we have accomplished and thus we come to believe this line of thought.

Man must be provoked into thinking more favourably about life.

He must be enlivened as to how lucky he is to exist.

So instead of being anxious about relationships and work, he pours himself into the universe and sets himself free.

Positive thinking encompasses this line of thought. Through thinking about how good it is to be alive, one is thinking positively.

We worry excessively in life. We worry about this and that and negate the astounding existential truths of existence.

We forget about our mortality. We forget that we are living on a planet. We forget about how lucky we are to exist. We do not see the chance that precedes existence as a human in this universe. The illusion we call life blinds us; it has made us narcissistic.

These existential truths are covered by our daily worries about finance, relationships, success, image, desirability, materialism etc.

We exchange our liberation for endorsement. Our freedom is bartered for desirability. Our sovereignty is overruled by retinas. All our anxieties lie in the eyes of others. We A) Observe how the herd lives and B) Determine what the herd wants and we mimic them to be endorsed. We are slaves to the eyes of our peers, our peers being the world on the whole.

The want to be loved or to be understood are just different ways of saying one wants to be endorsed. We seek the desire to be happy but our happiness is contingent on being approbated. If you stake your happiness on other people's perception of you, you play with dice.

Man lives in the dark and the dark universe can shine a light on his existence. The existential angst can set him free. Perhaps in the darkness he may finally see the light.

But it all starts with rectifying one's perception. To become free, man must alter his perception and then no matter what his situation on earth, he will become free.

If man can learn to worry, he can learn to think positively. If he can learn to cry, he can learn to laugh. If he can learn to chain himself, he can learn to set himself free.

It all starts with positive thoughts about life and being alive. Count yourself fortunate to exist. Think of the atoms of your body. Think of the neurons firing in your head. Think of the mighty universe the turns above and below you. Think positively about life and your life in general. Be grateful for just existing.

I once heard a person say that he wanted three things from life: To be happy, to be loved and to be understood. I told him to take away the need to be loved and the need to be understood and then all he was left with is happiness. You see he was staking his happiness on acclaim from others and hence the need to be loved and understood by others. This is it. We are programmed from evolution and education to see our redemption through others. We reject our naked self as viable and hunger for the universe to provide, when being alive itself is all one needs to be happy. If one loves themselves and understands the world, they can be as happy as they so deem.

It is most dangerous to leverage your whole self-esteem on success for what happens if the success vanishes. This is what people invariably do. A man is dependent on financial success for his mental wellbeing and a woman is dependent on her looks for hers. But what they fail to realize that the only certainty in life is change and when their success dissipates into the thin air so does their esteem with it.

Chapter 2

Entertainment

'Boredom or Entertainment?'

We must be entertained. We insist on being entertained.

Emotion is what we experience when we are entertained.

The human condition calls for time to pass quickly. The method of making time pass rapidly is through entertainment.

A good conversation is like a good film in that it makes people feel alive. It makes them feel enlivened and in being enthralled they feel emotional and in being emotional they feel good.

All facets of life serve to captivate man. Conversation, relationships, books, films, sports teams, food etc. They all strive to entertain man. The means may be different, but the end is the same: gratification.

We treat relationships like products that must guarantee satisfaction. We walk into the supermarket that is life and pick the best product, the product that most impresses us both unconsciously and consciously. We look at the product and like certain qualities but dislike other qualities and we accept or reject on this premise.

But this is one reason why we suffer because we insist on too much and when these desires are not met, we become distraught.

So modern day western man stipulates that he or she is in a relationship, they beg to work in a good job and henceforth bid to be happy. When these demands are not met, the individual reprimands his or herself.

When one goes to see a film, they request unconsciously to be emotionally satisfied. Failure to do so on the part of the film leads to a feeling of wasted time.

We demand the same of relationships. We unconsciously say we must be gratified to practise in them.

For the man, the woman must be good looking, funny, polite, intelligent. These qualities entertain him.

For the woman the man must be funny, be nice, be polite, intelligent, financially able. These qualities entertain her.

We measure people by their ability to beguile us and hence why good speaking is demanded because it entertains one unconsciously. We measure man by his ability to make money, make love, make history or make conversation. Seldom do we measure man on his ability to just be content. We are too greedy and request to be entertained with every second, every day and with every breathe we take. It is our biggest weakness, this want to be comforted.

We want too much of life and when these wants are not met we feel dejected.

The failure to achieve these demands makes us feel bad.

The trick is to be happy with your simple self. Be content in your own boredom. Enjoy your inner side. Do not want to be entertained at every given second of existence.

We use work, love, marriage, friendship, art, literature, sports and many more to make our lives worthy. They give meaning to our lives through quelling the boredom. But what is the meaning of life without these addictions and these escapes? There is no meaning. Man exists and he may as well just love his existence, every dying second of it.

Happiness

'Happiness cannot be bought, traded or earned.'

One either wakes up happy with whom they are or they are not happy.

What happens is man goes out to seek happiness and treats it like an addiction. He lives to be gratified. He is narcissistic. So just as an alcoholic gives into the demands of the drink, man treats happiness as a commodity which can be bought, traded or earned.

Thus, man believes that achieving in the world will bring happiness. He says that a successful marriage and job will procure the happiness that is so desperately desired. It does, but only temporary for the addiction soon wants more.

The want to be happy is an addiction. The drug addict wants heroin; the common man wants gladness.

He thus commoditizes his happiness and makes it an object. He merchandizes his life and everything in it. Happiness becomes job promotions and relationships and if he does well at these things, he says he is happy.

---Why relationships? Why do we have to be in one to be happy?

But yet again the happiness is only temporary in nature. Man feels happy for a period of time but then wants more and more.

This is the nature of addiction. It makes one want more. Enough is never enough. Thus, the man must keep achieving in order to achieve.

The cycle thus never ceases and transfers itself to his children. The children thus become a beacon to achieve more. They become material narcissists that must succeed in order to be happy.

The existential school of taught teaches one to just be happy with themselves. One does not treat happiness as addiction. One does not need to achieve in life. One does not need a high earning job or desirable relationship to succeed and hence be jubilant.

Ones existence in this universe should be a celebration, regardless of what you have or who you are.

In the existential school of thought man is happy just with his heart pumping blood.

In this method man can survive in all conditions. Happiness is found from within and is not dependent on external qualities to be realized.

The Zen teaches that man can be elated regardless of his situation. There is happiness to be found even in the deepest darkness.

There are two kinds of happiness: One is addictive happiness and the other is just happiness. Addictive happiness is all about gaining external reward from achievement. It is about being gratified. It is governed by narcissism. "When I look happy, then I will be happy," says the insecure individual. Happiness becomes something one must hunt.

What earning money gives is an addictive happiness. It is happiness that needs to be kept topped up just like car must be filled with petrol. It is temporary or acute. Real happiness is that which a person with nothing feels. True happiness is happiness without wealth. The fundamental wealth in life is wealth without money.

Chronic happiness is happiness that is found from within. It is being happy just to exist.

"Why can't I just be happy!" You are not happy not because your life is wrong, but because your attitude is wrong. You have low self-esteem because you tie your happiness to "looking happy." What is this "looking happy?" It is living the dream life which you can show off to your peers. In other words, your self-esteem is tied to how you are interpreted. You can do two things to alleviate this angst: Not care about what people think of you or secondly prevent them from interpreting you. My advice is do both.

"The trick is in what one emphasizes: We either make ourselves happy or we make ourselves miserable. The amount of work we do is the same." – Carlos Castaneda.

Happiness: You don't need to buy it, trade it or earn it. You just need to be it. If you want to be happy, just be.

The surest way of being happy in the future is to be happy now.

The capitalist happiness is pretence. People pretend to be happy because they follow a model of what happiness is generally thought to be.

The capitalist happiness is a template based on marriage and work. People thus think that if they placate this model they will be happy. But a lot of the time they are pretending to be happy because they have met the model that capitalism lays down.

We arrange our lives and thus our happiness from a very young age. We say in twenty years' time I will be married and will be at a certain stage in my career. We look to the future and say when I have this and that I will be happy. We think of our career but seldom think of our life. People are instructed to build a career rather than live a life. Sometimes to see forward one must look backwards.

Unfortunately, it often does not turn out this way because this happiness is based on addiction or gratification, wherein one must fulfil targets to be happy.

The only happiness is the happiness that comes from within. It is the happiness to just be alive. This is the existential happiness.

Think of the millions of women across the world who are obsessed with beauty. Make-up, clothes, plastic surgery, weight loss, you name it. They are obsessed because they want men to like them and when men like them, they feel good about themselves. It is narcissism. How does existentialism counter this? It says, stop being obsessed with making people like you and instead just be grateful to be alive in this universe.

Why don't the authorities step in? Why don't they say that people are narcissistic and will never become happy in such a method? They do not because this material narcissism benefits the economic system. When people attest that they will be happy once they have the family, the nice house, the esteemed job, the fancy car and so on, this benefits the economic system. They do not want you to be grateful and hence happy. They want you to be narcissistic and unhappy.

Image

'We are haunted by image.'

One of the most important drivers of society is our obsession with image. Economies are founded on image.

We unconsciously yearn to project a good image to the world. By world I mean those who know us. We are narcissistic be it basic or full-blown.

In conventional terms a good image is one that encompasses marriage and work. Image is a form of entertainment. It becomes an addiction.

Henceforth this is why these two qualities are held in such high regard.

We are at all times aware of whom we are unconsciously and we are always making inferences about ourselves regarding image.

A good image makes us feel good and that is why emphasis is placed on it. Happiness that is tied to image is a race that has no end.

It makes us feel good because people admire or respect those with a good image. Our lives are thus dictated by the eyes of our peers. Opinion moulds us.

This obsession with image is what makes us date, buy commodities and work. Often it leads us to date people we don't like, buy things we don't need and work in jobs that we get no satisfaction from.

We disavow what we really want in life in favour of things that prop up our image. Because of image we put demands on ourselves to earn the desired standard of life.

The profitability of dating websites and gambling institutions shows how obsessed we are with relationships and money respectively. Part of the reason we are infatuated with them is the unconscious desire to convey a pristine image. Relationships show we are in demand; money shows we are successful.

We measure others and thus ourselves by a threshold. The standard is relationships and work. Those who score highly project a good image, whilst those who fare poorly in relationships and work have a poor image.

One reason why we uphold the law is because we fear a negative image. We fear the eyes and judgements associated with being an outcast and hence why we conform indiscriminately. Conformity is the most common way to gain a good image.

We have at all times an idea in our head upon how we should live. So, we sit down and plan how we will live rather than standing up and living.

People are always making judgements unconsciously. They are narcissistic in nature.

---Will this individual make me look better?

---Will this job improve my standard?

Those two questions are image based. The person tries to improve their image or identity to their peers at the expense of freedom.

It just so happens that relationships and work are how we have come to measure ourselves and others. Hence when an individual fails at both they often get anxious. They do so because they are unconsciously aware that they are projecting a poor image relative to their peers.

Their peers may have a good life (good image) while they have a poor life (poor image).

We are programmed from adolescence to be competitive, especially those who grew up in a capitalist environment where they were given everything in childhood. Because they are used to always getting what they want when young they carry this want into adulthood. Alas it is much harder to get what is demanded when we are adults in the capitalist environment than it is as an adolescent in that same environment.

This obsession with presenting a good image is unconscious. We entrust a good image to our peers because it internally makes us feel good. Being wanted makes us feel better about ourselves. It is narcissistic in its roots.

This is why women go to such extreme lengths to look attractive and why men go to extreme lengths to be successful for it makes them more desirable and makes them feel good.

The problem is it becomes an addiction. Being sought after becomes a compulsion that we become a slave to and like all addictions we suffer in some way or form.

The individual in this case loses the ability to enjoy the simple life among other things. Life becomes a rat race of desirability that is commandeered by our unconscious fixation with image. Life becomes materialistic. The sufferers can only enjoy life when they are wanted and when this want dissipates so does the high associated with it.

Life is great when you are in demand. It makes you feel special. But what happens when this demand loses its potency? We become anxious and depressed because the obsession with image was an addiction that depended on one being highly sought after.

We are so absorbed in the system that we cannot see the cynical truth, that we are made insecure by the herd and by virtue of being known. When you socialize, what do you do prior to this socialization? You cosmetically dress yourself up. So, you put on nice clothes, or do your hair up, or put makeup on. Why do you do this? You do so that when you are observed you will be approved. But this is precisely why you suffer, because you are dependent on people to approve you, in order to approve of your individual self. This is called narcissism.

People want success because being successful affords them a good image. Their success is image based and not based on what the success actually is. A successful person is desired. That is why people want to be famous.

--- Why does one wish to succeed?

Is it because they love their job or because they wish to gain success for the sake of being successful?

Because of image too much emphasis is placed on friendship and not enough on solitude. Career growth is prioritized and freedom is ignored. Relationships are accentuated and existence itself is forfeited.

The solution is to just be happy to be alive. Don't be held at the mercy of other people's opinions. Be happy to be who you are. Be happy to exist in such a forsaken universe. Don't get involved in the material side of the equation. Be you a millionaire or a homeless person, be happy to exist. The greatest crime is in not being who you are.

All our anxieties and woes are in some way connected to people. The sick do not realize that the problem in life is other people. Guilt, shame or regrets all revolve around being labelled negatively by humans. We get told we can't live without people but we also can't live with them. Society is indoctrinated to believe that they must be in the company of others and fail to see that it is these others that cause so much distress. The problem is people and we believe that the solution is other people not realizing that this is just adding to the dilemma.

All our woes stem from being known.

Attractiveness

'We are all too easily seduced.'

Like conversation we are all too easily enticed by those who are attractive.

Again, just as good articulation sets neurons firing in our consciousness, those who are attractive looking do also.

We are programmed from evolution to admire those who are alluring. It is a weakness in our brain chemistry.

We thus choose people in spite of other flaws on attractiveness alone.

Another reason why we choose in terms of attractiveness is because it bolsters our image to others. Our peers will be impressed when they see us with someone who is deemed attractive. We are corrupted by narcissism.

That our respect will grow when our friends, family and peers see our attractive partner, means we ourselves will feel good because our image is in high demand and this makes us emotionally happy.

But again, like conversation we tend to ignore other damning traits in favour of dating or marrying someone who is attractive. Men will go for the woman who is deemed glamourous and women vice versa.

The dating game is no different from the shopping day wherein you buy products from the shelves. The mechanics and psychology is the same. We want a product that entertains us.

Our minds are automated unconsciously to do so out of sexual gratification and image primarily.

Take the man: He dates a good-looking woman. He thus gains sexual gratification and also earns from a desirable image amongst his peers. They will respect him more. This internally makes him feel good about himself.

Take the woman: She dates a good-looking man. She thus gains sexual gratification and also gains from a desirable image amongst her peers. They will respect her more. This internally makes her feel good about herself.

We chase the man or woman in high demand because they will enable us to externally gain respect.

Now there is a sexual aspect to it also in that we desire someone will allow us to achieve sexual gratification. But the external respect that we could potentially earn is what unconsciously drives us to chase the good looking individual.

Like conversation we are all too easily seduced by those who look good and we do not think things through.

Conversation and attractiveness should be used as qualities we look for but are not final by any means. But we are weak.

Furthermore, those who are deemed attractive are in high demand and hence we put ourselves in a bind with regards them.

---If I don't take him or her, someone else will.

We thus put unconscious stress on ourselves out of desperation to chase certain individuals.

The attractive nature of another puts us in a bind.

They say love is the greatest thing you can experience. It is not. Owning yourself is. Not being dependent on another person to make you happy is actually the foundation of maturity. From this stems your ability to engage in Authentic Love. It sounds so counter-intuitive, but it is those who are not obsessed with being in love that have the skillset to be in a relationship.

They say do what makes you happy. Often this is a contradiction because some people's happiness is contingent on making others happy and that is why they are not happy.

Never be desperate for someone. Never be desperate to be in a relationship because your desperation will make you do desperate things. Desperation makes you insecure. It makes you unhappy. The trick is to be happy alone as much as you are in a relationship.

In your worry to have a certain individual you will ignore other poorer qualities of that person.

Use attractiveness along with other qualities to judge an individual. It should not be the only quality.

Psychological Endorsement
'We live to be endorsed.'

Through systematic education when young we are thrown in at the deep end of the herd and forced to fend for ourselves.

Engaged in this battle we learned things. One of the things we learned was that gaining endorsement from our peers made us feel good.

As we grow up, we carry this methodology into adult life. When we accede to the demands of the herd, they are impressed and this makes us feel content. We thus learn that placating the herd at all costs is the means to live.

We live to impress others and through impressing them we gain psychological endorsement. Through obtaining endorsement we feel calm and soothed emotionally.

Children then carry this methodology of living into adulthood where the mechanism for life is founded on satisfying the demands of the herd. They are raised to be narcissistic and consequently to be insecure.

As such men and women live and breathe not of their own accord but by the goings of the herd.

Men try to be successful for that gains the endearing eye of the herd and enables them to be endorsed by the opposite sex.

Women live to be attractive looking so they too can be endorsed by the watchful eyes of society.

"When I am liked, then I will like myself," says the diseased individual.

It is a game that haunts people's lives. They can only be happy when the herd is happy about them. It says that the individual's existence itself is not enough.

What people then do is mortgage their self-esteem in being wanted (endorsed). They unconsciously say that when they are respected by their peers, when they are in demand, they will then be happy.

The system is exquisite in its propagandization. Nobody comes out of school or college and remarks about how they have been brainwashed for the last twenty odd years.

It is ridiculous how many have bought into (been brainwashed) that happiness is doing X, Y and Z. So many can only be happy when they are in a relationship, at a certain stage of their career, have travelled the world, have a family, found "the one," look attractive, drive a certain car, live independently etc. Why do so many intelligent people think like this, in such a pattern? They do so because they have been brainwashed to think so by the environment. Then they get a rude awakening when they have met the conditions of X, Y, and Z and are still unhappy. So what does the system do then? It prescribes them drugs and sends them to psychologists in order to take away their unhappiness and make them happy. Such people think like this because it is basic narcissism. Narcissism is saying: "I need." The theory is that if you can sever this narcissism, despite how miniscule it may be, you can actually become happy.

The insecure male or female thinks about journeying through life alone and such a thought haunts, poisons and to an extent kills him or her. He or she simply has to get married or else he or she is considered a failure.

Our biggest fear is not being killed or sexually assaulted. Our biggest fear is being known, it is being laughed at. But we are because of the system forced to expose our identity to the herd. This makes us anxious. What we then do to neutralize this anxiety is conform.

But it is a cancerous way of measuring one's happiness for it says the person needs to obtain external approbation in order to be content.

Billions of people thus live their lives in such a way that they live-to-be-endorsed. It is the very eyes of the herd that have one enslaved and if the whole world was blind we would be so much more liberated.

Heisenberg's Uncertainty Principle states that: The more you look the less you see. We cannot see the atom because when we try to look at it with a microscope, we disturb it. Likewise, the more absorbed you are in love and work, the less aware you are of the universe. The more you live, the less aware you are of who and where you are. This "economic narcissism" is vital for the system to function.

Self-Help Books
'Only you can change yourself.'

Reading books or watching films, observing others or listening to psychologists will not improve your life. Only you can improve yourself.

This set of notes will not change your life. To change yourself involves changing your unconscious. Consciously you may say you will change but can you convince the unconscious mind. Life will not change you; you must change life. There are the dreams of a better world and there is the desire to have a better one. We all dream, but seldom do people work for a better return

Change takes time. It is 99% perspiration, 1% inspiration.

Reading a self-help guide or listening to a speaker who talks about change will not change you overnight.

To change the unconscious demands to want other goals takes time.

It requires becoming more self-aware as an individual.

Solitude is a great friend of the self-aware. Through solitude you can reflect on your existence. You can start to observe yourself and what you do.

I would suggest that if you wish to change your life that you retreat for a period of time from life and try and find yourself. Go off travelling by yourself and learn to live alone. It is those who can live alone that have the skillset to be in a relationship.

Finding yourself in the Buddhist sense involves becoming one with only yourself. One does not need external gain to be elated.

Change, like happiness, can only come from within. The question is not what will change your life, but what are you prepared to do to change your life.

To change yourself you must change your instinct. If you change how you respond, then life will respond differently to you.

The good life is all a matter of perception. You can have nothing and the stars will twinkle, the sun will shine and the rain showers will become fountains of champagne.

It all depends on how you view life. Life stays the same but your perception of it will change. That is if you become one with yourself and nature.

Don't try and force your life. Force your own freedom and life will fall into place. Find your freedom; find your liberty.

Stress your own freedom, not your happiness. If one tries to construct their happiness they meet failure. Happiness must radiate from within.

Our lives are thus wasted chasing and giving into the demands of addiction. We waste our lives in pursuing a life we will never claim and don't realize it until it is too late. People say next year I will find happiness but they never do. The only happiness found in the future is the happiness you possess now. The seeds of tomorrow are sown today.

Ask Why and not What

'People know what they want, but not why they want.'

We know what we require from life. We want marriage and to work. We want to work five days a week and relax at the weekend. We want to meet new people and do exciting things. We want to be captivated by life.

People know what they want in life, but they are ignorant to why they want these things. People know how they are living but not why they live. People want the good life, but they cannot understand why they want it for they don't even ask why.

Man is dictated by his unconscious mind. This component of his psyche sees how others live and requests the same. It observes the rules of society and consequently pushes man towards them. So, man wants to marry not out of free choice, but because he is latently stressed to do so. A man wants work for the same reasons. Man meets friends after work or during the weekend because this is covertly commanded of him.

It is what behavioural economists call The Bandwagon Effect. We see how the herd behaves, we see how they live, we see how they become "happy" and we instinctively compute we need the same.

Man is not free. He is enslaved by his own instinct. He lives on instinctive drive of the unconscious mind and this plots his course with regards life. Man is living on this conformist instinct and that is why he marries and works. He observes how everyone else lives and unconscious seeks to mimic this behaviour.

Man is living the life of many. Life is repetition and a frozen memory. We are compelled to live in tandem with how people live. It is unconscious drive of the mind and not free liberty.

We know what we want but not why we want. We are governed by instinct but we cannot understand it.

Until an individual comes to understand why they are choosing as they choose they can never be free.

They are living in shackles. The chains inhibit their movement. They are not free.

To become free involves becoming more self-aware of why they choose.

We are so employed in life that we cannot understand what we do as we do it.

We are programmed on pure instinct and make our choices on instinct. Henceforth we live on instinct.

I meet so many who know what they want from life, but seldom do I meet someone who knows why they want what they want. We live on pure unconscious instinct and we do not know why we live.

All I ask of life's lonely martyrs is that they can generate the courage to ask.

Ask why you need what you think you need. Analyse yourself.

Nihilism

'Nihilism is freedom.'

The existential strain of thought can be a death sentence or it can be a release.

By teaching that man is naked against the universe, the individual in question can rebel against the shackles of conformity.

In order for man to gain his freedom, he must protest individually against the conformity of life. Man must escape internally and not externally. In escaping into himself without external aid, he sets himself free. Man must rebel against life. He must overcome his inherent narcissism.

There is no meaning to life. Life without man is still the same life we know. Man, through language tries to give meaning to life when there is none.

Man is simply an animal that can speak. The tool that man uses to see is language, just as a bat uses sonar to sense.

The world still exists without man to observe it. It is still dark and it is still mysterious. This is the nihilist stream of thought.

The existential nihilist believes in nothing. There is no meaning to life. Life is rudderless.

Life according to the existential nihilist is worthless and directionless.

Nihilism seeks to free man through educating him on the realities of the universe. Life is not about work or relationships; love or living. Life is simply about nothing and in this nothingness man tries to enjoy himself because enjoyment is emotionally warm to him.

Nihilism teaches that you are lucky to exist and one should try and make the most of existence.

Nihilism tries to unchain man from his addictions and his despair of existence. It tries to make him be happy with his life. Nihilistic love is the love one possesses just from being alive. To conform is to live and to die how everyone else lives and dies. Everything is observed and learned. We are taught to love, to hate, to want and to cry. If we are taught to conform we can teach ourselves to become free.

If you do not see life as a gift, regardless of who you are and what you have, you are doing it wrong.

Science fiction is already happening. We brainwash the young child through parents and education to behave a certain way and to want certain things. But we are so normalized on the system that we cannot see the system. We do not see the nihilistic nature of the universe. Women are told from a young age, make yourself as attractive as possible, dress a certain way, want certain things. Men too are told to behave a certain way. Both are blind to the universe and take their illusionary life for granted. The reality is that there should be nothing and we are lucky there is something.

They say if you don't have sex, you are missing out in life. This is just propaganda designed to make you afraid so that you will conform. You can be happy without having sex. The same applies to finding the one and starting a family. They make it seem that by not doing them you are somehow missing out in life. This makes the individual afraid and with their fear comes their obedience.

Existentialists like Sartre and Camus contend that man's greatest anxiety is associated with meaning in a meaningless world. I disagree. From what I have seen, most people are so caught up in the economic system of love and work and that is where their anxiety originates. Their anxieties are with respect to money, relationships, work etc. But existential nihilism can still be applied to this economic anxiety. You can enable the individual to overcome their anxiety through applying nihilism to their lives. This is the goal of Existential Nihilistic Therapy.

We teach our children that they need to succeed in order to be happy. We propagandize their minds on love and work. The reality is that existence in itself is the success.

Imagine a futuristic world so unbearable and so intolerable that a million of its inhabitants take their own life every year. We would think that such a world, such a system was absolutely terrible. How could any intelligent civilization adopt such a system, we would remark. Yet, frighteningly this science-fiction world is actually present-day earth. A million human beings commit suicide every year and most harrowingly of all we never blame the economic system that motivates them to.

Chapter 3

Childhood Indoctrination

'We have been indoctrinated from childhood on how to live.'

The life of one person is the life of millions. The mediocrity of one man is the mediocrity of millions of men. It's not the lack of success that troubles us, but our failure to achieve mediocrity.

You go to school, then post school, then college, then travel the world, then work, then raise a family, then retire and then die. Why are we all living the same lives? We do so because we were indoctrinated through the education system to behave a certain way. We are taught not to question the teacher and the teacher is life.

When we were young Santa was the lie. We grow up and we realize it was a deception. But when we were young we were also indoctrinated with the cult of conformism, only we never grow up to realize it is a lie. We grow up to believe there is no other way other than conforming to principles. When we do find out, it's more than likely too late. We are old and grey and the better part of our existence has passed by.

Education is indoctrination. Education conditions us to become addicts of conformity. Just as we have scientific models that explain the universe, we have models that describe how to live. Conformity is one such model.

When I was young I kept asking why I had to go to school. When I grew up I kept asking the same thing under a different tone. Why was education enforced?

Why do you think education is made mandatory by the powers that be?

Why are we so desperate to trust others? Why are we so desperate to be with others? We have been indoctrinated from childhood to believe that we must have others in our lives. We know of no other way to live because we have been bred this way like machines. No wonder they make education mandatory.

Education is mandatory because it prepares you for life. It teaches us to conform. It makes you dependent on others (friendship) to derive pleasure from life.

Because of education man is implored to live a life of conformity. Because of education he sees life as marriage and work.

The saddest part of life is that we dare not question it. We never ask: Why am I doing what I do? We simply accept the path that is laid out for us without even the faintest reprimand.

Education is necessary because the powers that be know that this is how one makes slaves out of countries.

This is how you transform them into machines. Through persuading them from childhood, they become inured in the system and know of no other way in which to live.

Education teaches them to become reliant on each other. It tutors them to work for reward. It disciplines them to think alike rather than critically think as an individual.

History has shown that those who derided the education system went on to achieve in life. This is because they were allowed to develop their own school of thought, their own voice rather than following the herd at all costs. Wake up before it is too late to.

The only education of substance is where the individual educates themselves.

Natural curiosity is the finest educator of all.

But because of the education system children are told to tolerate what they hear from others rather than question it.

99% of people on this planet are machines and will not achieve anything of note in their existence. They will just get up for work, work and come home and go to sleep.

We are machines that are simply coded psychologically to behave the same way, to achieve the same goals, to suffer the same mistakes. We are all the same.

We are all identical because the education tyranny has deprived us of the ability to critically think.

We become the soldiers of conformity who heed to the commands of the general and die ingloriously in battle and become forgotten.

I am more than ever convinced that the indoctrination of education when young is a large reason why men run into the battlefield of daily stress. Education has them duped and they cannot see their madness. They are blind to the truth that their friends, families and society on the whole has them in a bind. And I would argue that those esteemed patrons of society who have achieved more than the ordinary individual, only done so because they defied their education. People are not prepared to admit that they are fighting a daily battle.

The most important element of education is not learning to read and write or to count or even to enjoy oneself. No, the most important element of this childhood indoctrination is socialization and because of it the next generation grow up to all desire the same things in life of which economies on a macro scale benefit. They become inured on fellow people through this systematic brainwashing and hence we get marriages and work and many other qualities. It is not coincidental that the masses all unconsciously covet the same trades. They do so only because they are programmed to do so and not by their own willingness. Education despite what one thinks is what controls the masses.

One must remember that the true teachers of children in the classroom are the children themselves.

We are each nothing because we are indoctrinated to each be nothing and to enjoy this nothingness.

Lenin said he wanted to give power to the people. If one wants to give power to the people, don't systematically educate them. Let them educate themselves.

To control the people, educate them; to give power to the individual, let him educate himself.

Find your own voice before you grow old and lose it altogether. You achieve far more in life by being who you are and never letting others choose who you are. Own yourself above all else.

Capitalism

'Greed is not good.'

The capitalist ethos takes as much as it rewards. The two people who make a killing from capitalism are CEOs and psychologists.

One can earn money and achieve more than their neighbour and one may feel good about such a system but it has its downsides.

For instance, the capitalist agenda makes man much more competitive psychologically. He sees how others fare and he wishes to beat them because beating them makes him more desirable as an individual.

People become conditioned to earning reward as the currency of happiness, so much that most of their lives are spent unhappy because they do not reap enough to meet the standard of what is requested. They are told silently you can't be happy without money, marriage and work and sadly they believe what they are told. If you venture into the world to make everyone happy you will die an absolute failure.

Capitalism is a con-artist. It tells us things that are too good to be true and in our naivety, we believe them. The promised life is an illusion and reality is much bitter.

The capitalist is like a tree in a dense forest full of other trees. They all must compete for light against one another and the battle never ceases. Pure happiness is that tree that grows on its own in solitude and does not have to contend with other trees. It simply is let be.

We chase success because of what it affords us image wise. We can gain a greater image than the other individual. We are greedy.

Living for the sake of image is no life at all. Our lives are spent in pursuit of respect and love of the other. It is a game we take to our grave.

How is it that an individual who lives in a successful country and is successful in his own right can fall asleep unhappy? Why do the richest of the rich or the most successful of the successful still feel hurt inside? Why is it that despite living in a rewarding country that an individual will feel beaten?

I see this conundrum played out repetitively in the western countries. A man who has a degree but no partner is sad. A man who has a partner but no job is also dejected. The man who has neither is broken. No matter how cruel or despairing, a life is better than no life at all.

Contrast this with poorer countries wherein they are working on farms and have to make do with what they have got. They are happier despite not possessing half of what their western counterpart owns. Why is this? It is so, because of the ideology that is capitalism is missing. The people in the western countries are so used to having everything as children that they seek perfection as they grow up. This will to want progresses into their adult lives and when they are left in want they become beaten down with depression.

A child who has everything when young will seek everything as an adult. But the difference is in what is wanted. When we were young it was presents or trips to the cinema or sports match. When they grow up it is the pristine life that the capitalist template sets out and this template is: work, marriage and good social circle.

So, the individual ends up wanting these three things but they are much harder to achieve than the gifts when young. Thus, people chance their happiness on achieving in the job, relationships and friendship sector.

This is all fine if one does achieve in them. But if one does not achieve in them? They then start looking around. They see others achieving and they themselves are not. They then start to turn on themselves and beat themselves for not adhering to the capitalist agenda.

So, the problem is lack of foray in the relationships or the career they say. No, the problem is rooted in the capitalist methodology of living.

The capitalist methodology teaches one to be a certain way: To be a friend, a partner and a high achiever.

The capitalist methodology implores a specific standard of living. This creates the envy that spoils the heart of the person and when they then contrast themselves to another they either feel elated because they are better or they feel depressed because they are worse.

Pure happiness depends on not being envious of one's peers. Through not being jealous, one won't engage in a tit for tat psychological game of popularity. Pure happiness is when you possess nothing except your smile. That is a happiness that cannot be taken from you.

To be happy is to accept yourself on this planet and in this universe and to consciously be aware of what you are doing and why you are doing it.

If the means is happy, the end will be happy.

We get immersed in the whole living dogma every day that we become conditioned to it. Life loses its individuality and living becomes how everyone else lives. We read about friendship and relationships and see no other alternative.

The solution is not easy. One must become more self-aware of what they are doing in life. This involves vigorous psycho-analysis of oneself for an extended period of time in which the individual comes to realize that he or she is in fact living according to the template of conformism that capitalism extols. To escape the shackles of conformism one must understand why they are doing what they are doing. One is not working or dating because it is what that person wants to do. They are doing them because everyone else is doing it as well and this is what is latently demanded of us as people. The capitalist mantra urges conformity above all else to be successful and henceforth people unconsciously seek to conform because of it.

One must ask themselves a question: Am I living how I want to live or am I living how others want me to live?

"Others" in this case represents not only those who are known by the individual but also the whole world. In effect you are not free for you live the life of many. If you conform you are no different from the 99% of people who inhabit the world.

The capitalist ethos wants one to conform. It wants people to be greedy. It wants people to be envious of others. It seeks all these things because that is how that system functions and rewards the 1%. Being successful is a matter of perception. One does not need the house, partner or car. You just need to be happy with what you have got, which is a life.

Life becomes a pseudo-popularity contest wherein the goal is to be the most in demand of your peers.

Success and henceforth happiness becomes an addiction where people must reap their success and hence happiness to be jubilant.

Life becomes a shallow race. People want similar things as each other and they push each other to be more successful.

In effect a psychological bubble is formed wherein the people compete against one another to achieve the most and the happiness that is earned is only temporary in nature.

Someone may achieve greatly but the effect is like a drug that eventually wears off and another achievement is demanded to duplicate the feeling.

It is frightening how easy one is to manipulate. Look at how Queen lead singer Freddie Mercury was able to seduce his audience. Now apply that to conformity. We say a child becomes an adult at eighteen years of age. But for those previous eighteen years, that child's mind has been savagely indoctrinated with the cult of conformity. Happiness is ascertained to be relationships and work because we manipulate them to hold such convictions.

Man should only worry about food and shelter. Yet the capitalist mantra makes him worry about image, desirability, money and most of all himself.

The outstanding lie of conformity is that we cannot live on our own. We are unconsciously implored to seek out company. Our unique individuality is warranted as not enough.

The economic system makes people depressed, commit suicide, kill and yet we never think to change the economic system. Instead we change the person to make them more accommodating to the economic system.

Desirability means malnourishing our inner conscience. In order to be wanted we must compromise to our unconscious needs. At the expense of happiness, we choose stress.

Narcissism

'Narcissism is a product of environment.'

Narcissism is systemic in the capitalist condition. Narcissism is a huge reason why people are unhappy.

In order for people to survive in a highly stressful environment they must adopt a narcissistic façade.

This endeavours to harbour men and women who know nothing other than self-obsession.

Everything is about image to the narcissist. He works, marries and lives purely to uphold his projection to the world.

The narcissist is obsessed with image. It terrorizes his daily existence.

---How will they see me?

---How will this mix with the majority?

---Will my friends and family approve?

The narcissism is also a product of a harsh environment wherein confidence and articulation are the assumed skills. The narcissist front serves as a template to survive in a world where attacks and stresses are never ending.

The narcissist adopts the approach because he is insecure. Narcissism stems from a childhood of control. The narcissist as a child was subjected to dominance by a parent or perhaps both. He was used as a strut to further the image of the parent.

He thus learns that one must behave a certain way in the family to accomplish. He then carries this mentality into the real world of interpersonal relations.

The narcissist regularly changes his persona to suit the climate. When talking to someone he or she respects he/she is nice and submissive. When talking to someone he or she considers beneath them he/she dominates and discards them.

Narcissism is toxic. The individual sees others not as humans but as objects. He treats them as commodities in to which he can gain in the world. The narcissist demands more always and threatens to leave if his or her demands are not met.

The reason so many narcissists are observed in the capitalist economies is because they grew up with narcissistic parents and also because life necessitates that they be narcissistic. Confidence is expected in society. The narcissist is insecure by default and adopts the persona to survive. It is a cosmetic confidence.

The narcissist derides weakness. He deplores those whom he considers foolish or unsuccessful and often attacks them verbally. This apprehension towards weakness also manifests itself in his own soul. He cannot tolerate himself being observed as weak or easy.

I saw a video on social media, discussing how it is so important to work in a job that you like, because you will spend most of your life working. Similarly, it is so important to overcome narcissism as young as possible. What does narcissism say? It says: "when people like me, I will like myself." The prime example is the male or female who is obsessed with beauty. Why are they obsessed? They are because they tie their self-esteem to being labelled positively. When people like them, they like themselves. But it makes them suffer. They are so afraid of people and tragically so many never become happy, because of this inherent narcissism. They are both too immature and insecure to do so. They are drug addicts and image is their narcotic of choice.

Weakness is the ultimate weakness in the eyes of the narcissist and he feels those who are weak should be punished.

Narcissism corrupts. It does not matter if it's a relationship, friendship or work related. If the culture or individual is narcissism, you will be unhappy.

Traditional thinking espouses the notion that we need friends and a relationship to be happy. The reverse is actually true in that in order to mature you need to be able to thrive in your own loneliness. If you can survive alone, then you possess the skillset to have friends and grow a relationship. When I look at narcissistic people, I see the opposite. They need friends; they need a relationship; they cannot be seen alone. That they are so afraid of being alone, makes them insecure. This is why I remark that one should go off travelling for a year or even two, by yourself, because in doing that, you will teach yourself to live alone and hence mature.

The narcissist is to be avoided. His love is false. His feeling is a placebo. His kindness is reptilian. Often, they change once they marry for their unconscious realization that they now own the other individual serves to bring out the beast in them.

There is a faint hint of narcissism in us all and more than people cater for. We want to be admired by society and this urge, along with the need to supress the boredom drives our daily exchanges. This basic narcissism is detrimental to one's happiness. Overcoming narcissism is a huge step towards being grateful.

A young man despairs because when he goes out with his friends, they all manage to seduce a woman, but he fails. This man is insecurity personified. He has to be popular, he has to be good looking, he has to be having sex, he has to appear successful etc. in order to feel good about himself. Narcissism has infected his conscience. His happiness is contingent on all those things materializing. He is a gratification addict. So, what can he do? He needs to stop saying "I need" to be happy and start saying "I have." And the one thing he has that is his greatest wealth, is he has an existence in this universe. He needs to apply gratitude to his life.

Being known is the focal point of all anxieties in man. Classical thought dictates that people conform because they want to. So, men try to accumulate money and women try to look attractive. Existential thought says they conform because of anxiety. The fact that they expose themselves to society means they become afraid of the interpretation of that said society. This is basic narcissism.

Very often I see relationships in which the man is extremely nice as they date, but he changes once the contract is signed. This is because he is a full-blown narcissist and now feels he owns the other individual.

Often as well they attach themselves to inverted narcissists who are individuals who wish to be controlled and actually gain satisfaction from such an arrangement.

The narcissist father rules with an iron fist. Control and respect are the two facets in his reign of terror. Often, he makes threats if his wishes are not met.

The child thus grows up in chains. He learns that only by wilting to the demands of the parent can he achieve reward. So, the child grows up in the shadow of his parent's conscience and without his own liberty. He grows into a narcissist himself.

He begins to divide people into two: Those who are above him and those who are beneath him; those who must use him and those who can be used.

He commoditizes everything. His wife and children, his job and pastimes become mechanisms of which he can project a positive image to society. Often he is two men in the Jekyll and Hyde mode. He has his public persona and his private persona and they can differ radically.

Politicians are often narcissists. They project a public persona but in reality care little for their voting public.

A young man says: once I am a millionaire, I will be happy; a young woman says: once I look sexually attractive, I will be happy. Both neglect the present in favour of some future dream materializing and often waste their whole life being unhappy.

The root cause of narcissistic tendencies is exposure to the herd. That we are exposed to the herd when young, means we become afraid of how they interpret us. To neutralize this apprehension, we seek to conform.

The narcissist does not feel remorse. He is immune from remorse for remorse is weakness and weakness is despised.

Such is the illusion of modern day life that we don't realize how lucky we are to be alive. It is basic narcissism. "I can't be happy until I have friends; I can't be happy until I am loved; I can't be happy until I have the dream job; I can't be happy until I am rich." We just do not understand the chance that precedes human existence in this universe. The impression I get off people is that they believe humans have existed since the big bang and that they were intended to exist.

Narcissism is difficult to treat for it involves the individual acknowledging his own problem, which is considered weak in the eyes of the narcissist.

Narcissism is image based happiness. Such a person becomes happy when they see how positive their overall image is to the observing society. But it is a precarious happiness because one is afraid of what people think of them. Gratitude is a more concrete form of happiness and in order to profit from it, one must overcome their narcissism. In order to do that they must overcome their obsession with what people think of them.

To overcome narcissism and hence mature one must learn to live alone. They must learn to appreciate their own solitude. As long as they associate with people, they remain immature.

Gratitude should be the foundation of one's existence. Be grateful and then get married, start a family or work. To the insecure, narcissism is the foundation of their lives. They are not happy, but live to become happy through the accumulation of X, Y and Z. They don't become happy; they just want more and thus never become happy.

We spend our lives in fear of others and of ourselves. We are afraid to be who we are. Life is so simple and yet we over complicate it with our prejudices.

Money
'Money is the drug of the majority.'

We love to earn money and also spend it. Akin to conversation we have become addicted to it.

Money becomes an inclination. We become infatuated with making it and with spending it.

We chase money because of what it affords us in life, namely desirability in the image stakes.

The man who earns money becomes more in demand from the female point of view.

This is why he unconsciously pursues money. It improves his image. It makes him more popular.

The man is thinking of sex when he pursues a job that will pay well.

At the expense of his enjoyment he chooses money so that he will be high in demand and the females will want him.

He thus fritters away his whole life making money and then when his life is near an end he pumps this money back into his existence to try and prolong the final few months or years.

He is held in chains by his finance, by his own want to be desirable. He wastes his whole life in search of a better one and then it is too late to live when he finally learns to live.

Economies function on this want of money. It is a capitalist disease. It is greed and it is why capitalism succeeds because man can gain an advantage on others.

There are so many commodities that are bought purely to cultivate one's image. Man buys a car worth a fortune when a cheaper one will suffice to nurture his image.

Money is the parasite of capitalism. The want for cash becomes so strong. The more one earns the thirstier they get. It is like seawater. It is like heroin.

It endeavours to push men into a popularity contest. Those who earn the most get the rewards and thus life becomes a race to see who is the most successful. The most we accomplish in life is mediocrity simply because we quantify success in terms of sex and money, and history has shown that those who refuse to do this go places in the world.

The man chases the good-looking woman and the woman chases the successful man because they both stand to gain in some way from these templates.

The reality is that people don't actually know what makes them happy as Behavioural Economists assert. But the system tells them that conforming through working and marriage, will yield happiness. That people are so naïve and impressionable, they just accept this as true. Then one must apply the Easterlin Paradox to the equation. This says that the material life of money, work, relationships does provide happiness, but only to a certain point. That being super rich, does not equate to more happiness. Those who chase this material dream life get gratified, but the high wears off and they need more in order to feel good. The whole culture is narcissistic and one can never be chronically happy with narcissism. The trick is to be grateful regardless of your wealth or position.

What we are in life is decided by the opposite sex.

At the expense of individuality, we gain acceptance.

Thus, the younger generations are taught that life is about money. They grow up thinking the meaning of life is to earn money and earn what money affords us. The cycle of capitalism thus continues.

Gratification is nothing better than a drug addiction. Such an individual needs to experience a high in order to feel good. They become addicted to this experience. They need to have sex, they need to earn money, they need to buy some new commodity and so on. They hunger to be gratified. The pendulum swings between boredom and suffering. Gratitude is also a form of happiness but it is not a high. It is a maturity. It is a culture of gratefulness and one needs to mature to experience it. They need to overcome their narcissistic hunt to be gratified.

Adolescents unconsciously believe that life is a race. They become unconsciously programmed to see image as everything.

Thus, when they fail to project a good image they become anxious and depressed. This is the capitalist anxiety that accompanies conformism.

They must be taught that life is about love and not image. Money can buy you lots of things but not integrity.

People are led to believe that life is about earning. They must derive money, procure love and retrieve happiness. They are led to believe that one cannot be happy unless they have money. It is arguably the greatest deceit of capitalism.

Be you homeless or a lawyer your happiness depends on your perception of what happiness is. One does not need to earn to be happy. They can be happy just by being happy to exist.

This is what Buddhism teaches. Be happy because you are able to be happy. Life is a game of chance. The sun shines, the storm breaks.

We must make the most of every day, every minute and every second. Don't try to engineer the precision life but try to live the unbridled one. Your life is whatever you say it is.

One should always have goals in life, but these goals must be complemented by gratitude in order to be happy.

We cannot see the game. We cannot see the struggle. We cannot see how much we suffer just to make people like us or to maintain the fact that they like us. A young man spends most of his twenties and thirties in stress, building up a financial empire so that the woman of his dreams will lust for him. A young woman suffers to remain beautiful just so her husband wont stray. When you want people to like you, you struggle. Human beings, despite their dominance and intelligence are still profoundly unhappy. They waste their adolescence planning for their twenties, then in their twenties, they plan for their thirties, then in their thirties, they plan for their forties and in their forties, they realize that most of their best years have passed by. They only see the pattern when it is too late to do so.

Man is the only insecure animal alive.

Desirability
'Desirability is a disease.'

Man wastes his life in search of a better one. He misuses the better years of his existence in a struggle to make himself more desirable to his peers. We live to make ourselves more desirable and desist on the pure desire to live.

We desire to be liked and that is our greatest want, our greatest flaw. We want to be wanted. The man wants to be in demand from the females and the female wants to be in demand from the males and they both live in search of such want.

Desirability is the inured yearning to become more appealing.

The human condition is laden with this emotional virus.

Men spend their lives trying to be more worthwhile to women and women spend their lives trying to become more covetable to men. They are hopelessly engaged in a psychological war to make their identities more appealing to others.

Success does not have to be the annals of conformity. Success can be whatever you conceive it to be. It can be waking up into the universe every morning. It can be making money or living homeless. Conformity is but convenience. It is a system that is just convenient to our desires.

Existence is success.

Men measure their self-worth by the woman on their side and women by the man at theirs. Such a shallow existence I must say.

Don't look at life and try to cede to the pattern of conformity because everyone does. Look at life and find out what you enjoy and go your own way, your own path. Find your own calling.

Why is it that you yearn to be in a relationship or to be in a professional job? Is it because you enjoy them or because everyone else is doing them?

The human condition is weak. The mind wants to feel good about itself. The identity of an individual has a crack that commissions it to feel good when others like them.

Desirability makes us feel wanted and being wanted makes us feel good about ourselves. This is why we spend so much money and waste the entirety of our lives in a desperate attempt to become more eligible. It's a sad day when men and women still measure their worth in being wanted.

It first takes hold in adolescence. Adolescents enter into a pseudo-popularity contest which is based on who is the most advantageous. We want to be wanted and this drives us to squander our lives in search of this want.

Thus, the men want to be popular by being the sports star or the rich entrepreneur. The women want to be popular by being the best looking.

It is a chronic disease of the mind that inflicts most individuals. It can beat them down, but it can also implore them to achieve in life.

But the achievement is never enough. The call of desirability requests more. It wants more and when the individual can no longer achieve he falls into a crisis.

We feel down when we are not yearned for. We may feel envious when someone else is more desirable than ourselves. It is a sickness. It is a game, a sick game. Do not waste your life trying to be better than everyone else. It is a race you cannot win.

This want is the fulcrum of capitalism. The desire to be better than your neighbour or peers is what turns the crankshaft of that materialistic ideology.

The atom could not exist without Heisenberg's Uncertainty Principle and without atoms there would be no Kim Kardashian. The average man and woman know everything about their chosen profession, but they know nothing about two distinct things: The universe and their place in it.

Capitalism is dependent on greed and desirability is greed personified. It is why new technologies are spawned because men and women want to triumph more than the other.

Desirability is an addiction in that the feeling that accompanies one being desirable makes one feel good and the individual thus is consumed to hunt this feeling repetitively.

We all want to be happy, but we all measure our happiness equally. There is happiness and there are the "labels of happiness." One is the appreciation to exist in an unforgiving universe; the other is based on obtaining certain materials to be realized. In chasing happiness, we ultimately chase the labels on the basis that upon reaching the designated target we will be happy. So when the individual gets the marriage, the job and the mortgage-free house, they contend that they will be happy in the eyes of their peers. But the chase never subsides and we grow old and despair at all the times we felt unhappy.

The most important component of this insidious education is not the teaching of subjects but the fear instilled into the mind of the young child. Essentially, they get taught that unless they do X, Y and Z, they are failures, who will be humiliated. Thus, they learn to possess a checklist of things needed to be happy. You need friends, you need to be in a relationship, you need to be having sex, you need to be popular and good looking, you need money, you need fancy commodities and so on.

But failure is destined to occur. What happens when we grow old and lose our looks? What happens if the business fails? What happens if we get ill?

Desirability works as long as you are desirable. When you are no longer in demand, the pain will rain down.

One must grow up and see that all they need to be happy is themselves. They don't need to be coveted. It is a benefit if one is in demand, but one's life need not revolve around it.

All one needs in this world to survive is food and a positive attitude. Don't be held ransom by the opinions of others. Don't be held in the guillotine by desirability.

Happiness must flow from within. One is a partisan to their own delirium.

Success if anything is being who you are in a world that wants you to be someone else.

Relationships/Marriage

'There is no such thing as perfect partner.'

On forums in particular I often read the following:

---I'm still looking for that certain someone.

Instead they should ask:

---Why is it that we automatically believe that we have to be in a relationship?

---Why is a relationship usually of two people?

---Why do I measure my happiness in terms of relationships?

These entities are models that we have come to use in life as the standard. In the same vein that we wear certain clothes for certain occasions because that is social etiquette.

We are hindered by moral etiquette that commands that we have to date and furthermore only date one person at a time. It is neither right nor wrong. It is just a model we have unconsciously adopted.

We spend so much time trying to have a relationship with others that we forget to have a relationship with ourselves. We are instructed to have a relationship with others at the expense of having one with ourselves.

Yet most people's lives are at the behest of this model.

They are told by others that they can't be happy until they are in a relationship or married.

They then unconsciously come to adopt this reason.

They convince themselves that their happiness lies in relationships.

They are guilty at dreaming of the future and not living in the present.

Look at how football fans are manipulated to spend fortunes supporting a football team and apply that to relationships.

We treat relationships almost like a career. It is something we have to work on. We crave to be entertained. Relationships are poisoned by their own wants. It's like we are going in buying a new shirt and we pick which one suits us the most. Which shirt makes us feel good about ourselves? Without language there is no relationships. Nothing. A relationship is like any addiction in that it is something we have manufactured to pass the time.

The future promises reward in a marriage. The "true love" will make me happy they say. Marriage won't make you happy. If you are not happy now, the chances are you won't be happy in the future.

They have become indoctrinated in the whole marriage fantasy just like the religious fanatics are indoctrinated on their chosen faith.

I have come to regards the ideal that is marriage and the promise that happiness lies on its green pastures as a form of fanaticism.

We become hopelessly habituated on its idealism that we cannot live content by ourselves. Many people thus waste their lives chasing the perfect life when the perfect life is simply being alive.

The only happiness you will find in the future is the happiness you have in the present. Buying into this religion that is "true love" and "the perfect marriage" is foolish. It is dogma espoused by parents and peers.

There is no such thing as the perfect marriage or the perfect life. We must compromise in some way or form.

We are all seeking the same qualities. We all want to get married because we are told our salvation lies within it. It becomes our redemption. We are drugged on its fantasy to the point that we can't see the realities of existence. Marriage is a form of social control.

We are also put under pressure by friends and family to marry. There are hidden demands that we must abide by. Friends all put stress on each other to conform. Families also expect their children to bend appropriately.

Are we independent or are we just machines? Love or marriage is the system that economics uses to breed new humans.

The human mind does show pattern. People are raised in the same methods and thus think in the same logic. We all thus desire the same things from life because we are indoctrinated from youth by this capitalist mantra that says we have to behave a certain way to be happy.

The whole world is brain dead and is hooked onto a life support machine that determines how they live. There is no freedom or independent thought. If you were free you would see how you live and ask why? Part of the problem is we spend too much time talking and not enough time thinking on our own.

You don't need meaning to be happy; you need gratitude. The quest for meaning can make one suffer, particularly if your meaning is motivated by narcissism. People in their naivety chase family, chase money, chase careers, chase this dream life, that they think will make them happy. All they meet is anxiety, despair and boredom.

Commoditized Relationships
'We treat each other as objects.'

We are a slave to our own addictions. We want sex but don't want to feel used. Henceforth we developed this model called relationships.

But the minute a man treats a woman as a means for sexual gratification, she becomes an object. The minute the woman treats the man as a means to improve her image, he becomes an object.

There are a lot of commoditized relationships. They are a distinct product of the libido of capitalism. Commoditized happiness is fickle. It can reward but it can rain. Pure happiness is not.

The ideal relationship is where you have nothing except each other. There is no image conscious appeal or making the family/friends happy. It is unbridled happiness for each other's company. Authentic love comes alive in solitude where the participants are silhouetted against the treacherous existential landscape.

Relationships in the capitalist world are like a trip to the grocery store. We walk in to the grocery store but this store is different. On each aisle are potential partners who we can choose. We look and look and scavenge through the aisles until we find a most suitable partner.

This is what people do. They look for the potential partner with the best qualities just as you buy the computer or coffee machine that impresses you most.

A commoditized relationship is a relationship we are in because we need to be seen in one. It is governed by narcissism. "I will look good when people see me with this person." It is an insecure relationship.

Think of the person who needs to wear the expensive clothing. They need it because they need to be seen wearing it. Just as they need to be married and have children, so that people will see them as such. The whole culture is narcissistic. It is about making people approve of them and that is why they are deeply unhappy.

The mechanics of how you choose a partner and how you choose a car are the same. They are both commodities that you purchase and you buy them on the premise that they are of suitable quality.

The capitalistic ethos has commoditized relationships. They have become products wherein we look for certain aspect of the potential partner just as we look at the certain parameters in a technology.

We don't realize it that we look for aspects of a potential partner just as we look for the most economical product on the shelves in a shop.

In order for Authentic love to thrive, those in the relationship must distance themselves from the herd. Insecure love or commoditized love is where you date a person who makes you look good in front of your peers. Who are your peers? Your family, friends, co-workers and neighbours. In order to engage in Authentic Love, you must distance yourself from these people.

Ironically in order to engage in Authentic Love, one must banish this obsession with True Love. You have to mature and become grateful for existence on an individual level. Once you become happy with just existence itself, you possess the skillset to build Authentic Love with the person you like. The common error I see is that the person states that once they find love, then they will be happy. Maturity is the reverse: You are happy from the get go and from this stems your ability to build a relationship with someone.

I remember seeing a thread on the internet about who was the most attractive person people knew. Most people were saying famous people, like actors or sports stars. One woman said it was her husband. She made two very interesting points. One, she said that she was surprized he showed interest in her initially. What this conveys is that this woman had low self-esteem issues regarding her perceived appearance. Secondly, she said that she loves when people comment about how she "snagged a good one." What this conveys is that the symbol of the relationship gives more pleasure to her than the relationship itself. This is a commoditized relationship, which is a narcissistic relationship, which is a diseased relationship that one enters into to retrieve admiration. I felt sorry for both the male and female in this relationship. For the male, because he is basically being used as a PR stunt for his insecure wife to procure applause and for the female because of her low self-esteem she lacks the maturity to actually engage in a relationship. All in all, to engage in Authentic love, you must distance yourself from the herd. This woman was so afraid of being laughed at by the herd that she became insecure. What she needed was to get off social media and distance herself from her family and friends. To put it bluntly, if her husband had the same personality, the same confidence, the same qualifications, the same financial success, but lacked the good looks, she would not have been with him. She was mainly with the man so she could show him off, like a gold medal around her neck. This is symbolic of a commoditized relationship.

We depend on others and other things to make us happy. It is a dangerous game for it says that the individual alone cannot make him or herself happy. People should do away with these mental checklists with regards a potential partner and just try and enjoy themselves.

Who got laughed at in school? It was the person who was not popular. It was the person who was not sexual. It was the person who did not have the correctly labelled commodities. This makes the individual insecure and they carry it on into adulthood. How do they neutralize this insecurity? By being sexual, by being married, by having children, by owning extravagant commodities etc.

I remember reading about a woman complaining that she was miserable. Why was she miserable? It was not because she was in pain or homeless or in debt or unemployed. It was because she didn't have a kid, a high paying esteemed job, a house etc. She looked at all her friends, who had families, houses, holidays, good jobs etc. and felt she was missing out. This woman was insecure, most likely because she was narcissistic. She had been taught by the system that happiness was the accumulation of X, Y and Z. What she needed was an existential therapist to pull her out of her diseased mentality.

In order to be mature which leads to gratitude which leads to happiness one must overcome narcissism.

Learning to live alone is probably the most important skill that you can acquire on your path to being grateful.

Friendship

'Friendship inhibits us.'

Family and friends are considered the cornerstone of life for many.

They provide support and love unconditionally.

But what people fail to realize is that it is friends and family that put us under unconscious stresses to accomplish in life. This is most certainly the case if friends and family are narcissistic.

People are cast in an invisible bind just as a planet is stuck in orbit around a star. We cannot see this bind but it exists.

It is friends and family that make one conform. It is friends and family that make us self-absorbed with image.

Paradoxically it is friends that constrict our freedom and it is our very enemies that make us rebel, the moral being that to fully revel in your succulent freedom your need more enemies and few friends.

We are so afraid of a negative judgement from friends and family that we approach life as if we must impress our friends and family to be of worth.

People thus live under the shadow of their friends and family. What friends and family require is extoled and the individual refuses to be their own beacon of light.

We live our lives as determined by the covert requests of what friends and family demand. Furthermore, we are unconsciously put under duress by family and friends. We want to impress them with who we date and who we are.

They expect us to conform as in they expect us to marry and work in a certain job.

It is because we are covertly demanded to meet certain parameters in life that we then become absorbed with image.

That we are commanded to behave a certain way then puts us under pressure to improve our identity image wise.

We then unconsciously become consumed by projecting a good image. Our lives then revolve around image augmentation. Our image must always be improved. What it is now is never enough.

This is a feature of capitalism. People are devoured by hidden races to be the most desirable and it all stems from the invisible threats that they are saddled with by friends and family.

It is the opinion of friends and family the implore one to live within the constraints of conformity. We look to others for strength and reject our inner strength.

Work backwards. People with social media accounts finely tune their profiles to earn validation from the viewing public. Now apply that to your life outside of social media. You finely tune your identity to earn validation from those who know you. Who knows you in this case? Parents, friends, neighbours, co-workers etc. This is narcissism, be it basic or full-blown.

What education and parenthood do is compel us to mature relative to the economic system. In other words, when we have friends, a partner, children, a nice job, a car, a nice holiday every year and so on, the system says "well done, you have succeeded. You are mature." Then because the individual has spent twenty, perhaps thirty years indoctrinated by the system, they cannot see any other way of life. They are mature with respect to the economic system, but grossly immature with respect to the universe.

Our lives, our relationships, our jobs are determined by family and friends. They dictate how we live.

Happiness dependent on another is not certain. If you place your happiness on another you play with dice.

We fear a negative judgement from friends and family and this unconsciously manoeuvres us to bend to the will of conformity. It is the fear of labelling by friends, family, peers and partners that causes so much anxiety. This silent threat implores is to conform. Our anxiety lies in their eyes. All our woes stem from other people. To be known is a death sentence.

All our anxiety comes from the eyes of others. That we are known by others condemns us.

The anxiety associated with labelling is one distinction between man and animal. We are unconsciously aware that man can and may label us.

The job you work in, the person you love and the life you live are all decided by friends and family. Don't work in a job for money or status. Work because you enjoy working. We get told to build a career but not to live our lives.

People thus don't live their own lives. They live how others wish them to live.

Nothing in life is perfect. No choice or ideal is 100% fool proof. What friendship gives you, it also takes away. Because of friendship you unconsciously must live in the shadows of others.

Desperation

'We are unconsciously desperate for the good life.'

People generally believe what they want to be true, not what is true.

Our youth is wasted on others. We want to be adored. We want to be in a relationship so we can say proudly that we are. Conversation has tainted our nerves and made us toxic to individuality.

A retired pensioner with money to invest and with the threat of inflation looming tries to put his money into schemes that will grant a return. Often they throw their money into Ponzi schemes in their desperation.

Their unconscious impetuosity for something to work out means they will believe the scam.

Life mimics this process.

People are desperate not to be single and hence they throw themselves into poor relationships in the belief that they will work out. We are so rash to live that we end up not living. In our hopelessness we believe our salvation lies in relationships. In our carelessness we marry without due diligence and marry into discontent marriages. Instead of freedom we choose the will of others. We choose melancholia because of the opinions of our peers.

The young female sees her parents married, all her friends married and all these celebrities enjoying life married and she then gets it into her head that she needs to be married to be happy. The environment frames it as the idyllic necessity that you need to be happy. This is false. You can be happy without marriage.

People are desperate to work in image promoting jobs and hence slave themselves for the opinions of others.

The profitability of casinos and dating websites shows how desperate men and women are.

Man frantically desires to be wanted and forfeits a life of contentment to be wanted because in doing so he gains a temporary happiness.

We want the good life not because of the good life but because of what it affords us.

The man looks at his bank balance and remarks that if he does not find a suitable wife, he will be missing out in life; the woman looks in the mirror and likewise remarks that if she does not find a suitable husband, she will be missing out in life. Both of them are afraid. They are afraid of not living life to the fullest and that is precisely why they are not happy.

We have been so intoxicated on the virtues of the good life that anything other than it is deemed a failure.

We look at others and observe their achievements and then look at ourselves and witness our own failures. This is called Social Comparison Theory. We are always comparing ourselves to others. To mature we simply must stop doing this.

We use the good life of conformity as the litmus test of whether we are "living."

There is being in love with someone else and being in love with life itself. It is not enough to love another; one must love life itself. To love another one must love life itself.

Living thus becomes image oriented and not about true happiness. Our lives are like stage plays: Every act is rehearsed and every word is scripted. Man lives as if he will live forever and dies having never really lived.

The individual wants to be approved though and their desperation to be acknowledged makes them seek refuge in the herd. They are afraid of being negatively judged by the majority and thus fall into the grasp of the crowd.

Man is caged by the opinions of others and so long as one seeks solace in the herd one will never be free because the herd will undermine how one lives, acts and speaks. To escape the herd, you must not become known for it is those whom you know that cast judgement on you. To be known is to be condemned and to be condemned is to be known.

Because of image we unconsciously ascertain whether we can benefit from a certain person. Our daily relations with others are dominated by whether we can gain from them image wise or entertainment wise. This is narcissism.

We gain appreciation when others see our immaculate image and this must be upheld to remain pleased.

People thus chase and chase in life. They hunt the good life and become so desperate to have it that they do not live. To seize the day is not enough, one must seize their existence.

It is wrong to do this. Just be happy to exist. Do not chase life, let life chase you. Do not be anxious for the good life that secures your image. Just be happy to be able to be happy.

Our lives reek of despair. We are hasty to earn money to live and in doing so we refuse to actually live. Each moment spent unhappy is another inch of your life vanquished.

The hunger to find love and work this dream job, makes us insecure, but because the economic system is so dependent on both these things, this hunger is not labelled insecurity. It is labelled as normal behaviour. When you complain about failing to find love, no one says, that the search for love is futile. They tell you to keep searching. Likewise, when people suffer stress at the hands of the work component, no one says, we must change the system. Instead we drug the person to try and change them to become more accommodating to the system. The other interesting point is that because the system is so entrenched in the individuals mind, they cannot see the true reality of the universe. The universe may as well not exist because the illusion of life we call the economic system causes the individual to be blind to it.

You will never achieve much in life if your wants are the same as everyone else. Want what few want, desire what few desire, live how few live.

Our wants are our weaknesses and they fail to live up to expectations. The man says when I have this job or this woman "my life will be good." The woman says when I get this man, "my life will be good." It doesn't work that way. What you are doing is dreaming and not living. There exists a great disparity between fantasy and reality. You can't chase life. You just let it be and it somehow chases you. He who rejects today in favour of tomorrow died yesterday.

The Paradox of Hedonism

'The more you chase happiness, the less happy you get.'

Happiness cannot be bought, earned or traded.

Man wastes the better part of his life chasing a better one. You won't find life through chasing it. You just have to let it be. Man spends half his life searching for a better life and the other half dreaming of a better life. We don't live our lives, we hunt our lives and there is a difference.

The paradox of life: We suffer not because of suffering but in want of a better life.

We are led to believe that if we adhere to the parameters of capitalism that we will become happy.

So we plan our lives ten or twenty years in advance and ignore the calling of everyday essence.

The problem with this type of living is that one cannot strategize happiness. One cannot look to the future and say that if they have this and that, that they will be happy. Don't go looking for life. Just let it be and it will come to you.

Happiness is like sleeping. If you try to force yourself to sleep, you will lay awake all night. If you just relax and dream you sleep comfortably.

Chasing happiness won't find you happiness. One must just be happy. Pursuing the ideal life won't get you the ideal life. Man looks at the stars dreaming of another world, a better world, when the one he is standing on is the only world. There is no other life, no other universe. This is the only life one has, so make the most of it.

Happiness is spontaneous. The more one chases it the more elusive it becomes. The more one tries to enjoy themselves the less they do. It is a contradiction. If you try too hard to enjoy life, you will not enjoy it. The common man says I will go out now and meet a few friends and enjoy myself. But he never does. You have to be happy from the start.

Paradoxically it is those who can tolerate their solitude that can love more.

I have found that the faster you chase and the harder you want, the more unhappy you become.

If the destination is happiness you will never reach it. If you try to achieve happiness you will not be happy. The journey is the destination and the destination matters not. We wait for life to give; when we must give to life.

Thus, in life one must not live to achieve, but rather live to have a good time. Through relaxing oneself in life, one enjoys life all the more.

The only happiness that conformism bestows is an addictive happiness that is derived from success. If the individual achieves in life, they feel a sense of reward; they feel gratified. But it is short lived for the feeling subsides and it needs to be topped up. They are too immature and narcissistic to be grateful.

This is why so many in capitalist economies are anxious ridden. Their happiness is dependent on external factors for its fabrication.

The only true happiness is the happiness that comes from within. You won't find love if you are searching for it. You won't find the dream life if you want it. You have to just be happy. You need to have an attitude of gratitude.

Thus, the people who plan their happiness in the future fail to be happy in the present. The only happiness one finds at the destination is the happiness they brought with them through the journey. Happiness is the journey.

It is the people who don't chase success that gain success. The people who don't go looking for the ideal life, that live the ideal life. The people who want happiness rarely get happiness.

Your essence is your success.

Happiness is not an external commodity. It is internal. It bleeds from your soul. To enjoy costs money, but to enjoy your own existence costs nothing.

People who grow up in the capitalist economies are used to having everything. In gaining commodities they earn a temporary happiness that vanishes after a while and needs to be replenished with another commodity after a period of time.

Every avenue of happiness thus becomes commoditized. A book, a film, a match, a relationship etc. all are external commodities by which someone becomes intoxicated on happiness. It is a cat and mouse game of achievement, as in as long as one accomplishes they will remain happy. But what if the achievements cease?

The surest guarantee of happiness is to be happy from within rather than going out looking for happiness. The only happiness found is the happiness you discover inside your soul.

Those who try to gain happiness from the world rarely do. Don't chase happiness, just be happy.

You cannot be happy, you can only experience happiness. So many naïve, insecure and immature people remark to themselves: "Once I have this or that, once I have X, Y and Z, once I have the good career, the good partner, the good house and so on, I will be happy." You will not become happy through such a method.

If your happiness is material, you will never become happy. What you get is a high, like a drug addict gets off their choice of drug. But the elation wears off. It is like seawater, in that the more you drink, the thirstier you get. This happiness is cyclic: You buy a new product or you succeed in some way and you feel good. But the high subsides and all you are left with is either boredom or eagerness to experience the high again.

Schopenhauer said that the pendulum swings between boredom and suffering. If you apply a narcissistic analysis to this proposition, it means that the individual suffers to be gratified, becomes happy, but the high wears off, which leads to boredom, which then leads to one "suffering" to become gratified again. The solution to this mechanism is gratitude and the method of applying it is to become more tolerant of your boredom. Instead of yearning to become gratified, replace this hunger with gratitude. When you inject gratitude into your boredom, you will find that the hunger to be gratified reduces. Teach yourself to live alone without the so-called luxuries of life. Then you will become grateful and hence become happy.

One should not approach life to gain in it. They should approach life to have a good time.

Through not chasing life, they find life will fall into place.

There is the want of happiness and there is just being happy. One is consciously chased and never gained. The other comes like the sun rise.

We are so preoccupied with trying to live that we don't live.

People firmly believe that happiness can be obtained.

---If only I was in a relationship.

---If only I worked in that job.

---If only my life were this.

They commoditize their happiness and think that it can be worked for. It cannot.

What invariably happens is the anticipation of happiness is far greater than the actual happiness. What we dream of, is always more seducing than what we live as.

Again, this anticipation of happiness stems from the capitalist ethos and it is a poisoned way of thinking.

We automatically think we have to earn our enjoyment from external sources such as another person or film. This leads us to become anxious when we do not receive happiness.

The surest method of happiness is to just be happy to exist. We are lucky to exist in this flicker of time and light we call life. Be grateful for your existence, every drop of it.

Happiness is often linked to the unconscious mind. One cannot consciously try to be happy. One cannot say to themselves: "I will be happy now for the next two hours." By doing this they distract their unconscious mind from working.

In order to be happy one has to almost escape into another world. Through immersing themselves in another person or thing they allow their unconscious mind to experience either pleasure or pain. If it experiences pleasure then happiness occurs but if it experiences pain, unhappiness of occurs.

For example, when watching a film one becomes immersed into that world. One allows their unconscious mind to be manipulated by the screen. If the film is good the individual feels happy unconsciously. If the film is bad the person does not feel content. Now apply this logic to a conversation with another person. One escapes into the other person in a sense. If the conversation entertains the individual feels good. If it does not entertain the individual feels dejected.

One cannot thus plan happiness because to do so is the consciously try to gain it and one cannot do this. To be happy one must allow their unconscious mind to be provoked.

Thus, saying to oneself that marriage or a career will yield happiness is a faulty proposition, for the more you expect to be happy, the more it will elude you.

The means to be happy is to immerse yourself in life and hope that you become happy through doing this. So you meet friends not under the pretext that they will make you happy but rather you just meet them for a bit of enjoyment.

If one marries to become happy, they won't. If one works to become happy, they won't. One cannot say from the offset that they will be happy through doing a certain thing but rather they enter into the moment not expecting much and the moment can produce happiness.

"Life is more than just existing," said a man. This is precisely why he is unhappy because he has to "live" in order to be happy. We actively teach him for the majority of his youth that "living" and hence being happy, is falling in love, working the esteemed job, having friends, being sexual, owning fancy clothes, a fancy house, a fancy car, going on two fancy holidays a year etc. This type of happiness benefits the economy and hence is extoled. This man is completely oblivious to the fact that he is alive in a universe and I don't blame him, for this is how we coded him when he was young. This man had a lot of maturing to do and it starts with just being grateful for being alive. The only thing you need to be happy is the correct attitude.

In essence all you can do is escape unto life and hope that this escape yields happiness but it is not guaranteed.

Of course, if one is happy alone they increase the odds of being happy for they are not dependent on people to make them happy. If one is dependent on people to make them happy they must allow for chance because people are irrational and unpredictable.

Addictive Happiness

'We become addicted to feeling happy.'

There exist two types of happiness: Pure Happiness and Addictive Happiness.

Addictive happiness is a happiness that is based on reward. It is gratification.

If one achieves in life they feel relaxed emotionally and this feeling is good.

This is all good until the feeling subsides and the individual must succeed again in order to earn the same relaxing feeling.

The only problem is that the next success must exceed the previous one or else the typical high that is felt is not established.

Thus, the person in order to be jubilant must go out into the world and accomplish in life and they must obtain more each time.

But when they get more, more becomes not enough such is the nature of addiction.

The mechanics of all addiction is the same. The means differs but the end being the reward is identical in feeling. One feels good after they succeed.

This is a poisoned happiness for it says man cannot be happy until he has triumphed in life and consequently man becomes so habituated in his addiction that he believes happiness can only be retrieved in this concrete world of success.

Man is for this reason held at the mercy of his addictions.

The other happiness is pure happiness or gratitude which needs no material success to be found.

Pure happiness is one where man wakes up each day grateful for his existence and consequently his perception of life is altered.

He no longer is held accountable to his desires. Instead of yearning for happiness he is simply let be and finds a calm gladness from within.

It is a happiness that does not need exterior qualities for its existence. It is a happiness that is borne from the inner soul. It is a happiness that comes from simply being alive.

People instinctively live on addictive happiness. Through growing up with everything they become unconsciously bound to success as a means to be content in life. It is an addiction just as a heroin addict's life revolves around his drug of choice.

Furthermore, they strategize their happiness. They plan their lives twenty years in advance. "When I am married, I will be happy; when I have that career, I will be happy." They neglect being happy in the present, in favour of this narcissistic dream of happiness in the future. This is called Strategic Happiness. It is a product of narcissism.

Sometimes you must think backwards to see forwards." What am I doing, rather than what will I do?"

Success becomes the drug, when life itself is the only drug you need. Your essence is your success.

It is a mechanism of the economic system. We romanticize life for the individual to make him or her give consent and become a parent. We do not teach him or her about the worthlessness of life, we do not teach them about the nihilistic realities of the universe he or she inhabits, because those things are not romantic and will not lead to him or her giving consent.

To endure in this universe is a miracle. To be able to realize we exist is another miracle. Just be grateful to be alive. That you are alive is your success. Success lies in inimitable obsessions.

We are the most intelligent animal in this universe, but for what intelligence gives, it also takes away, in that we are also the most insecure animal in the universe. We are human, all too human.

Chapter 4

Change

'To change your world, you must first change yourself.'

Change is not easy. It involves training your unconscious mind to rid itself of its desire to conform.

One is not consciously conforming. It is unconscious conformity that endeavours to make you live the common life.

We live on instinct most of the time. A conversation is driven by instinct. A drive through the streets is controlled by instinct. Our lives thus are governed by instinct.

Through adolescence and coupled with the capitalist ethos we are convinced that we can only be happy when we assuage to the will of conformity. We can't be happy until we are in a relationship and have a good job. It is a disease.

The greatest deception is self-deception. We come to believe that we are living by our own conscious choice when our life is moulded by the environment.

To change yourself you must thus train your unconscious mind to respond differently to given situations.

One way to do this is to become self-aware of your reactions.

Imagine for instance you were driving and nearly have an accident. After the event you would conduct an accident report. You would consciously look at why you nearly had an accident.

---Was I driving too fast?

---Was I not paying attention?

---Were the roads icy?

This is what one needs to do with their normal lives. They need to analyse their behaviour. Our lives are accidents of which we do not analyse. We just accept how we live and do not question our actions.

We know what we want from life but we don't know why we want it. We want to conform but we don't know why we want to conform. We just do it unconsciously.

Change thus can only be brought about when you come to accept that you are conforming in life. You are behaving as others behave because you are unconsciously programmed to do so. You live as others live, you covet what others covet and you want what others want because you are unconsciously ushered to do so.

You measure your success on conforming.

How many ego-centric men and women understand the laws of quantum mechanics which govern the atom? Without these peculiar laws, there would be nothing. Forget about having sex, making money and finding your "soulmate." Start thinking about how lucky you are to be alive in this universe. When you do this, you mature.

To change this cycle, one must become self-aware. They must accept that they are living in response to the echoing's of conformity.

They should ask:

---Why do I want to date?

---Why do I want to work in the professional job?

And above all else ask:

---Why do I want to live as everyone else lives?

The truth will set you free if the truth is you realize you are imitating unconsciously.

Through accepting their plight and becoming self-aware they can then change their unconscious requirements through conscious manipulation.

By consciously telling oneself that they don't need to conform they train their unconscious mind to become more accepting of the failure of not reaching the requirement of conformity.

Through this they become unconsciously free.

Their lives no longer revolve around the addiction of success. Success becomes just waking up every morning.

They no longer give into their addictions to feel alive. One should feel alive for just being alive. They no longer go out to chase the world. They find that just existing is enough enjoyment for them. It can only be done by becoming self-aware and it takes time.

There is no quick fix or solution. To become self-aware involves perhaps two or three years of psychoanalysis. But slowly one begins to train their unconscious to perceive differently. One trains it to react differently. Happiness cannot be merchandized; it must erupt from your core.

Use your failings as your strengths. If you are alone, embrace the loneliness. Use your weaknesses as your glory. Use your vulnerability as your power. If you are penniless, embrace it. If you are nothing, espouse the nothingness.

You can always choose the reaction. You can always choose how to respond. Be happy just to wake up every day. Be grateful to be alive in a universe that is indifferent and forsaken.

The common world rarely changes you. It is you that changes you. We wait for the world to change us. We wait for marriage and a good job to make us happy. Only you can change you. You may not be able to change your condition but you can change your perception and when you have changed yourself you can try to change the world.

Gratitude requires maturity and maturity requires gratitude. They both work off each other. The more mature you become, the more gratitude you convey; likewise, the more gratitude you convey, the more mature you become.

It is narcissism personified. Such a person's whole life revolves around conveying a better image than the other individual. I knew a woman once who epitomized this narcissistic anxiety. She had to have a boyfriend; she could not bear entertain the thought of not having one. She had to look attractive; she could not bear entertain the thought of being unattractive. She had to conform to what society expected a woman to be; she could not bear entertain the thought of not being a "woman." Her eyes, the very organ that gave so much to her, were in fact killing her, because she was afraid of how people interpreted her. In an existential sense, she was not a woman; she was a fashion.

Self-Learning
'Learn to listen to yourself.'

We get taught everything except how to learn ourselves. The only thing you need teach someone is how to learn.

Curiosity is a great gift. Richard Feynman once said that curiosity was the real prize of life.

Curiosity is the pleasure of discovering something for yourself.

Curiosity or self-learning is the pleasure of living your own life devoid of the opinions of others. It is not what you learn in life but how you learn. You can spend your whole life solving what has already been solved and that can make you feel like a success. Or you can have the curiosity and patience to try and solve that which has never been solved. Natural curiosity is the finest teacher of all.

Very few people listen to their own soul. Very few people are self-aware to the point that they know what they are doing in life and why they are doing it.

People are so drugged on life that they don't know why they are living.

Thus, they learn how others learn, they solve how others solve and they live how others live.

One should never be afraid to learn by their own hand. They should not be afraid to live and thus learn their own way.

Instead we are taught to live an identical existence and as such we die an identical death also.

Education is not being taught; education is teaching yourself. What lies circumferential to us is nothing compared to what lies within us.

People need to approach life on an individual level. There is too much following like sheep and not enough leading like wolves.

People all too readily accept the life ahead of them. They accept what the teacher tells them is final rather than coming to their own conclusions.

One will never gain in life through wilting to the eyes of others.

We end up in pursuit of the same qualities in life rather than living our own distinct life. We are pressurized to speak. Is the silence of our pure existence not enough?

Man must learn to live his own way. He must learn to listen to his own reason, his own heart and his own soul. Existence itself is the quintessential romance.

He must learn to live through himself and not replicate his behaviour because others do it.

Does the average man or woman understand the big bang or the quantum theory of the atom or the strong nuclear force? No, they have no knowledge of these things. Why? They don't because they are taught when young to prioritise sex and work above everything else. We don't teach them about the chance of the universe because if we did, they would question what we call normal life. It is all an illusion. There must be trillions other planets in the galaxy and you won't find love and work in any of them.

Very few men answer their own calling. Most men yield to the calling of many men.

If you know yourself and you know the world, you may never fear the rising sun.

The world is a slaughterhouse and man its doting meat.

Regardless of what you have or what you do not have; who you are or who you are not; your existence in this universe is a cause for celebration.

Buddhism

'We are what we think.'

Buddhism teaches man to think for himself.

It imparts to man to become more aware of his existence.

It communicates to man to be happy just to exist. People spend most of their lives trying to find happiness when all they have to do is simply be happy from within their quiet soul.

Hunting happiness is like chasing a rainbow. The prize at the end always eludes us.

Our lives are wasted on the premise that we are immortal and that is why we die without ever having lived.

The Buddhist nature is one where man forgoes the common capitalist race and starts to become one with himself.

It is without question the most beneficial religion.

Instead of believing what everyone else believes, man is urged to listen to his own heart.

The wrong reason to do anything is that you need to be seen doing it. That is narcissism.

Man thus formulates right and wrong, genius and criminality not on the scriptures of conformity but based on his own reason.

Through Buddhism man is encouraged to see where he has followed. He is implored to think by himself. He is commanded to live his life on his own terms and not to unconsciously follow what others wish him to follow.

Man does not need wants or gains to be happy according to Buddhism. To be happy all he needs is happiness.

This is why the happiest people come from the most impoverished parts of the world. They are content just to survive each day. Their foes are not other people or ideals that they must facilitate in order to succeed but rather their foe is the weather or hunger.

In the battle for warmth or hunger they become alive and forget about trying to appease others.

The enemy as Buddhism teaches is not the individual who achieves more or the individual that hinders a man's way. The enemy is the individual himself who through his own thoughts gives birth to capitalist reptiles of the mind. If you are going to teach anybody in the world, teach yourself.

Man is inhibited by his own conscience. It is his own thoughts that sow the seeds of destruction. His own mind inculcates him to chase life rather than live life.

Man becomes institutionalized on his fellow man. He comes to survive on his fellow man so much that he cannot survive by himself. Courage is not lack of cowardice, but being true to who you are.

Happiness can only come from within. It cannot be discovered in the hearts of others. It comes from man's own heart, his own thoughts and his own freedom. Don't wait your whole life for happiness; just be happy your whole life.

Happiness depends not on objects, but on how you think. If you can have everything and not be happy, you can have nothing and be happy. It is all perception.

Man's own worst enemy is himself. His own being inhibits his happiness. Man is his own beast and his own god.

Man's salvation can only come from amid his soul. Expecting the world to change you will not happen. Only you can change you. We expect our gains to make us happy but they become addictions that need to be serviced. It is only from being happy at the start that we can be sure of happiness at the end.

Love your life: Don't go out to live. Go out to love and you will live regardless. Don't go out to enjoy yourself, go out to be yourself and you will enjoy yourself regardless.

All I ask is one becomes more self-aware of themselves. This entails comprehending what they do and why they do it.

Do not try to conquer the world but rather try to conquer yourself. Be in love with each blink of your eyelids, each glorious day you live to see.

Existential Freedom

'Be happy with whom you are.'

You are so blessed to be alive. You are even more fortunate to be able to realize you are alive. Life is precious and yet we are in want of a better one.

Capitalism poisons our perception. It says we can't be happy until we earn. This is the lie that your unconscious mind has adopted. We become habituated to others and come to believe our lives lie in them, when our salvation lies within us.

Just be happy to be alive. Be grateful for your ability to open your eyes and see the world.

Existentialism teaches man to come face to face with the realities of the universe. We are all born in the abyss and we must reach the stars by ourselves. In doing so, he can redeem his liberty and escape the shackles of daily existence.

Man's life is two dimensional. He sees the blue sky but fails to see the light being refracted to make it blue. He sees the stars but cannot comprehend how far away they are. He sees himself and does not realize the atoms that make up his body.

You can purge a lot of anxiety in life by stopping trying to be liked in order to be happy. I see so many ambitious individuals whose sole purpose is to be approved or be lauded.

What is the meaning of life? There is no meaning. You exist. You are lucky to exist. You are even luckier to be able to acknowledge your existence. Make the most of it. Love life and it will love you back. Love every synapse of your calling.

Man's life becomes about love and work. The other aspects of his existence are relegated to insignificance.

Life becomes about image and material gain. People focus on relationships rather than reality. They spend time talking rather than thinking. They live on instinct rather than conscious thought.

Thus, all our problems have common denominators. We are either failing at relationships or we are finding our job stressful.

Existentialism or Buddhism endeavours to teach a man about the harsh facts of the universe.

If man can only open his mind and see the supernovas or the planets revolving around the stars he may negate the angst that daily life throws up.

So instead of gazing at the stars on a cold night wondering where it all went wrong with life, perhaps our lonely man will come to realize how precious life really is and will start to radiate the happiness from the inside rather than trying to absorb it from the outside.

Your body contains cosmic relics from the creation of the universe. Almost all of your hydrogen atoms were formed in the Big Bang, about 13.7 billion years ago.

There is so much freedom in the angst. The universe can set you free. Existence can be both your executioner and your redemption; it just depends on your perception.

The amount of times I have read about someone who says that they look at their friends or peerage on social media, who all seem to have good lives and they wish they could have the same. Three things spring to mind: One, we are all the time comparing ourselves to others. This is insecurity and immaturity. Two, we think that if only we had this or that, we would be happy. This is false. The person has narcissistic insecurities that prevent them from being happy. So even if all their dreams came true, they would still be unhappy. They need to change their attitude, not their life. Three, if you are constantly comparing yourself to those on social media, what about those you know in real life? Your friends, co-workers, parents, relations and neighbours all put you under pressure to obtain X, Y and Z, in order to be approved and hence happy. The moral being, you need to distance yourself from these people in order to be more secure.

I am not suggesting one disowns their parents or friends, but one must be prepared to defy them. The other thing to remember is that if your parents or friends are narcissistic, then you will be narcissistic too and will suffer.

We have to keep selling ourselves and that is a huge reason why we are unhappy. We have to keep making people like us.

I am not suggesting that one should avoid relationships altogether to be happy. What I am suggesting is that in order for the relationship to be healthy, both people in the relationship must be mature. They must not be narcissistic.

Change your perception of what is happiness. Change your means of life and you will change the end. Loving others first starts with loving your naked existence.

Become existentially free and release your being into the world. Become one with nature. There is no destination to happiness. Happiness is the journey. Be addicted to your own freedom. Find your own liberty.

The best psychologist in one's life is oneself. If you cannot change yourself, no one else will. No amount of books, work-shops or people can change your ways; only you can do that.

Acceptance of yourself and of your limitations, are the first two steps on the path to change. If you can live in your own solitude, you can live anywhere.

Poverty

'There is much wealth in poverty.'

Man is conditioned to believe that poverty is alienation and that greed is good.

Poverty becomes a symbol of failure in the eyes of the capitalist.

But poverty can be positive. Poverty can make an individual appreciate how good life is.

We live in a society where we have everything and perhaps we have too much, that in order to feel alive we must want more and retrieve more.

Our daily existence is centred upon an addiction in which we need to triumph in more in order to be happy.

In poverty are found some of the happiest people on earth.

They are happy because they are thankful to just exist on this planet or this universe.

They are happy because they don't compare themselves to others and don't feel envious of the good life that others live.

They are happy because they find warmth in the simple things in life such as a cup of coffee or a simple conversation.

Cynicism can release a man from the stresses of life. If you can see yourself standing on a planet as you live or if you can see your atoms that make up your body you may just be happy to exist. We need more cynics in life.

Man is so distracted from this existential cynicism through gratification and the unconscious conquests of life. People negate the realities of the universe through relationships, friendships, sports, art and work etc. But they go too far in those addictions and when the addictions are not serviced, they suffer. They feel anxious. The goal is to feel free as you accept how insignificant your life is. There is much freedom in the cynicism. Life finally reveals itself and man begins to see himself and his existential worth. We are all blind and only the existentially aware can see themselves.

Those in poverty are happy because they wake up each morning thankful for just waking up.

They are happy because they can find the positives in the rain storm as much as the heat wave.

People take their existence for granted, particularly their privileged existence. In order to appreciate life more people need to try poverty and to see how lucky they are to possess what they possess.

We are corrupted by romanticism. That is why most people fail at life.

Poverty can be a great example of how to love life more. So instead of endeavouring to find love in life, one learns to love life instead. There is so much wealth in poverty and so much poverty in wealth.

If you love life, it will love you back. Do not follow the "road" to happiness. Just follow your own soul, your own calling and your own being. You cannot conceive happiness; it must drain through you.

The westerner is schooled on greed. Every facet of his life becomes a race. Why the need to achieve in life? Existence is the achievement.

This Capitalist Game Theory is never ending for the individual. Every day becomes a battle to improve his stock and when he is successful his stock rises.

But every sun kissed morning is filled with dread and anxiety.

There is no greed in poverty. The only anxiety is the age-old anxiety of will I survive this day.

This is how the homeless survive. Their daily existence is simply about warmth and food. They have no anxieties over image and success.

It is a tough but simple life and they appreciate the food they earn far more than the capitalist.

You either "become happy" or you are happy and the former is a disease of narcissism.

True Love

'There is no such thing as true love.'

We expend our lives searching for something that does not exist. Love plans for tomorrow but life lives for today.

We get inured on conversation so much that we can't do without it and good communication skills are extoled.

We get duped into working at jobs we hate purely so we can be seen to conform.

We get indoctrinated to believe that we have to be in a relationship to be happy and thus come to understand that no other path to happiness exists.

It is this latter point that gives birth to this charming deceit we call "true love."

It does not exist. It is a product of man's ability to speak and if he could not employ the tool of language there would be no such thing as true love. Language, without it there is no such thing as love.

Does it exist independent of language? It does not. It is a poisoned dream spawned by the principles laid down by conformity which we unconsciously must adhere to.

We automatically assume enjoying ourselves is sex and money but why not solitude and love.

One must also see that we are all the same. Psychology and economics would not exist if we were all so special, as we are led to believe.

People grow up in adolescence convinced of their own worth to society. They believe that because they have a distinct name and face that they are special. They are not.

We are all the same personality wise. We all make the same choices. This "true love" is a great illusion of man designed to give meaning to our lives. In looking elsewhere for love we refuse to love ourselves. A diseased individual says they need to be loved before they can love themselves.

Modern existence is a work of exquisite science fiction. The shrewdest component of this science fiction is that we don't realize it is science fiction. In this modern dystopian world, we pollute the mind of children through parents and education. We impregnate their minds with romance propaganda so that they will spend their whole lives searching for "the one," or "their soulmate." We seduce them to work for the reward of money and the good life. Any behaviour that does not advance the system is outlawed. People become slaves to money, sex and image. Those people who struggle to conform are prescribed drugs to take away their anxiety and unhappiness and enable them to contribute to the system. It is a hybrid of Kafka and Orwell in its operation.

Authentic love is not this one magical thing that you must experience and is not your sole purpose on this planet. It is a profession. It is not a romantic feeling. That is the mythical true love that people are indoctrinated to believe when young. There is no "the one," or "the soulmate." What actually exists, as in authentic love, takes hard work, patience and maturity. Consequently, those who believe in true love and hence search for it, are too immature to experience Authentic Love.

There is probably some intelligent alien life form from another galaxy writing about a dystopian world that is exactly what we humans call life.

People are not one in a million or one in a billion. No, there are millions of people who are all identical.

We treat love as ownership. We must own the other individual. Nobody owns or possesses anyone. We just formulate agreements and truth be told we are born alone, we live alone and we die alone.

People must learn to see the great deception that is this romantic jargon we call love. Life is cynical and indifferent. Before you were born you were unknown and when you die you will be condemned to be unknown.

Individually love is worthless; collectively it benefits economies. True love is the biggest prostitution ring in the world.

What exists is Authentic Love. I would strongly recommend that you read Erich Fromm's The Art of Loving.

Human beings excel at perpetuating myths. True love is among the finest of these. This concept that there is one person in the universe designed to complete you is madness. All we are is trillions upon trillions of atoms woven together; all we are is an animal that can speak. This one person you are supposed to discover and build a life with does not exist because true love is a myth. To be frank, those who buy into the ideal of true love are still extremely immature. They are still in the adolescent phase of maturity.

Love is like happiness. The more you want it the less you get. Don't love another person. Love your own life instead and you will love another person.

Foolish love says I need to be loved to feel love. Intelligent love says I love therefore I will be loved.

Immature Conformity is tying your happiness to possessions. In other words when you have the partner, the family, the house, the car and the dream job, you will become happy. Mature Conformity ties your happiness to your existence. That you are alive is cause for celebration.

Narcissism must be supressed in order to be mature and hence happy. Stephen Fry was correct when he said that what unhappy people have in common is they keep saying "I need." This is narcissism be it basic or full blown. "I need to look good; I need the latest gadgets; I need to drive a fancy car; I need money; I need to be married…." This is why narcissists (even those with basic narcissism) are never happy, because they yearn for more and then when they get more, they need even more.

Animals may worry about food and predators, but they don't worry about "not living" or "what people think of them" or "not being happy." We are more intelligent than other animals but often not as secure.

Yourself

'Your only enemy is yourself.'

People are immune from blaming themselves. If they should fail in the world it is always someone or something else's fault.

They accuse everyone except themselves. It is either man or nature who is at fault for their miscarriage.

You are the master of your destiny. Only you can decide your fate.

The world is predictable. People all live the same way. They all craft the same errors and mistakes. It is up to the individual to see this and to act accordingly.

The individual that demeans you is only yourself. It is your own conscience that forbids you.

The capitalist narcissist has grown up used to receiving every luxury that when he fails he vents is anger externally.

The world is supposed to fall into his arms and kneel before him he believes.

Our lives are made more uncertain with the more people in our lives. To plan your own life is tough enough. To be reliant on others to make ourselves complete is madness.

But this is it. Through capitalism and pseudo-narcissism we have become conditioned to believe that only through others can we be happy.

The group is extoled and the individual is derided. Obedience is demanded and creativity is ridiculed. We lie awake sleepless because of the past or future and the beautiful present lies unperturbed.

But this very dependence on others to be happy is also the reason why we fail to find happiness.

We become held ransom by others to gain our passion. We are at the mercy of their minds. We become the planet that is held in orbit by the bright star and without that star the planet is inhospitable.

The problem is we are too afraid to go alone and because of this we construct our enjoyment at the behest of others. Our friends become our only source of passion and it is a dangerous relationship for what happens when the friendship turns sour?

You cannot understand quantum mechanics because you as a human being cannot see the effects. Likewise, you cannot understand the effect of being known because you are so socialized to be known. Meeting people in this world is second nature.

Man is his own worst enemy because he becomes habituated unconsciously to believe that he can only survive in the group and he pours all his chips into this so-called friendship. If he can be led to believe that his salvation lies in others; he can be taught to survive on his own.

You are your own worst enemy because you put yourself in a bind psychologically. If you can dance in dark, you can dance in the light. Man needs to be encouraged to go alone. Man needs to rebel against his own unconscious to change. But we live in society that quietly demands friendship and overtly ridicules solitude. But who cares what they think. It is your life and not theirs.

Do not betray your most prized gift: Existence.

The goal of life is to love your life.

You will not live by wanting to live.

The Future

'We are too busy dreaming of the future that we forget the present.'

We contemplate our lives ten or twenty years in advance so much that we refuse to live in the present.

A man is dreaming about success when he is nothing. A woman prepares for her marriage in adolescence.

Our lives are arranged, then wasted and seldom lived.

We are so busy dreaming of a better life that we disregard the present.

Man must try and live each day of his life. He must live each second for what it is worth.

But man lives the present in a drugged-up delirium of the future. He is all the time probing for a better life when the one he has is good enough.

He becomes doped on the riches of capitalism and the greed of success. He rejects himself as a failure not because he is a failure but only because he has not succeeded in the methodology that capitalism demands.

Each day should be greeted as success; each second we are alive should be our affluence.

People are blind and capitalism has a habit of holding a blindfold over its citizens. They can't see the sun, the stars and the great dark universe. Life becomes about relationships and work and they must achieve at both.

Capitalism produces an anxiety of the heart of which existentialism is the anti-dote.

Plato was right but for the wrong reasons. We are condemned to spend our lives searching for our other half. But we only do so because we are addicts and of the conviction that we need to escape into another to person to be alive. We are brainwashed on conformity. Life is "other people" we are led to believe, so much that we cannot tolerate our own loneliness at all. One does not need what they think they need. Relationships, jobs, sports and art, they are all just means of escape. What people need is a mirror to see how they live and to see themselves escaping from themselves. So great is life that we are condemned to run from it.

Do the Kim Kardashians of this world wake up and exclaim that quantum theory of the atom is a beautiful and perplexing theory? No. She wakes up thinking about how good it is to be Kim Kardashian. With respect to the economic system, Kim Kardashian is a god. She is worth millions. With respect to the universe she is an outcast.

You will never become happy if you yearn to be happy the next week, or the next year or the next decade. What you will do however is waste your life suffering to be happy. I think the economic system is partly at fault here, because it promotes the illusion that by having X, Y and Z in your forties and by using your twenties and thirties to accumulate X, Y and Z, you will suddenly become happy. Then they reach their forties and are left standing in the rain. "Where is this happiness I was promised?" The trick to being happy in the future is being happy in the present.

Life is both the venom and the anti-venom to existence for it all depends on how you perceive it.

Remember Santa Claus or the Tooth Fairy when young. You were taught to believe them. You also get told when young how to be happy. It consists of doing X, Y and Z. Such is the indoctrination or inculcation, that you cannot envisage any other existence.

Some people waste their whole lives in search of that elusive rainbow we call happiness and thus fail to dance in the rain that is the essence of every day.

But waiting for the storm clouds to pass is futile for one must find solace in the rainstorm. One must enjoy the present to enjoy the future.

The more you try to force yourself to be, the more you destroy your true self. In wanting to be someone in the future we reject who we are in the present.

The individual who must get married is absolutely terrified of existence. Life to such a person is not a gift but a penalty.

You are standing at a junction. To your left is marriage and family; to your right is solitude. You can only choose one route. The mature person is happy to pursue both options. They can go left or right. The immature person can only go to the left and that is why they are unhappy.

Stages of Life
'We go through the same stages.'

Despite what we are led to believe we are all the same.

We live indistinguishable lives and make the same choices.

Part of the reason we make the duplicate choices is because there are so few choices of which to choose from. It is either: Conform, non-conform or criminality.

Because we exhibit the same thinking we all go through the same stages of life.

---In adolescence we go through the popularity phase.

---As we enter our twenties we go through a pseudo-popularity phase.

---We then mature as we hit our thirties and decide to settle down. We think of starting a family and continue our jobs.

---We then grow old and finally mature and see life for what it is. But it is all too late. The truth has only dawned far too into the autumn.

The time to observe the truth is in the spring, so that you can maximise the return of the summer.

But we only see life for what it really is when we are in our elder years.

We only come to realize that we wasted our summer years conforming to an overused and under lived calling, the calling being conformity.

When we were young we were sure the summer would never end, but unfortunately it does and it progresses rather fast into autumn and then into winter.

People are clueless to these stages. Life is just life when they are living. They fail to see themselves and others replicating the same pattern in their lives.

They become convinced in the summer that life is marriage, family and work and the summer has no other calling.

That we are able to see stages is ample proof that people conform. They live the same lives as everyone else. Their calling and their soul is the same as everyone else's.

We do two primary things to the young mind that make it seek relationships. A) We threaten them with a negative label. So parents, friends, co-workers etc. all say latently that if the individual is not in a relationship, they will be ridiculed. This threat has a huge bearing on why they are so desperate to find love. B) Secondly, we instil an insidious guilt within them. We effectively say that if you don't find love or your "soul mate," you are missing out in life or not experiencing life. This guilt is a huge incentive to find a partner. The individual is naïve. Relative to the economic system they are mature; relative to the universe they are still childlike in maturity. In fairness to society, many figure it out, but tragically when it's too late, as they are in their elder years.

The government does not have to force society to conform because society forces itself. The culture is self-inflicting or self-perpetuating. It is parents, teachers, doctors, politicians, celebrities etc. that inculcate the young generation to conform.

We are born alone, we die alone and in between we live alone. But if man can learn the authenticities of his world and himself, he thus becomes one with himself and enjoys the world more. Our salvation is autogenous. Before you find someone else you must first find yourself.

If the goal is to be happy, be happy to exist under the pale moonlight of this universe. Society is taught to be narcissistic. Go around to the schools and colleges and you see students who say: "I can't be happy until…." I can't be happy until I am rich, smart, have sex, married and so on. This is why they are not happy and this is why they will never be happy.

I cannot repeat it enough. Stop trying to be liked. The man who chases money and the woman who spends fortunes on clothes and cosmetics, do so for the same reason. They want to be liked. But paradoxically this is why they are unhappy because they need external endorsement to be good about themselves. This is narcissism.

I have no issue with those who realize this truth and make a conscious choice to live that way. But what of those who are blind until they are old?

It is when we are most alive that we are most convinced that life will never end.

Be grateful for your existence. Your success is not your achievement in life but the very fact that you have a life. You are not born existentially mature; you must become it.

The Universe

'We cannot see the universe.'

We live in the dark to the realities of life.

We are so captivated in life that the fact that we are living on a planet that revolves around a star is hidden from us.

We are so drugged on conformity and image that the greater solar system with all the planets is ignored.

We become so conditioned on work and relationships, on the nine to five and the friendships that as we live we forget about the dark despairing universe.

In the midst of life, we are blind to the universe.

This is the cusp of Existential Nihilistic Therapy. It tries to rid man of his capitalist anxieties through making him aware of his essence in the universe.

We unconsciously know we exist but this life is based on the two dimensional rules of conformity. We only see other people and the blue skies. The vast disheartening universe is hidden from sight and our daily lives are centred around day to day repetition.

If people can unconsciously begin to understand the universe they live in, if they can see the stars and the black holes, they can gain a new lease of existence.

Freedom is the lack of day to day anxieties that accompany living.

Existentialism sets out to try and make people free. Through understanding how lucky they are to exist and how even more lucky they are to be able to realize they exist, people can escape the shackles that accompany conformity.

The universe may be inhabitable but it is glorious. The dark depths of space can expose a man. Be in love with yourself above all else. Love your own universe.

Man is so lucky to be alive and yet he fears life. There is so much anxiety in living. Life is great but living is painful.

The existential theory sets out to liberate man and the limitless universe can do that. You must cry for your individuality. You must realize how lucky you are to be alive.

The night stars can make a man dream. People will fail to be happy so long as they continue to ignore the vocation of the universe. Own yourself and you will own the universe.

Don't do what everyone else is doing. Don't live how everyone else lives. Don't be a slave to opinion and desire.

The way the light dances on your retina; the way the sound flutters in your ears; that you can live and be free, this is your finest achievement. Your existence is your glory.

The problem in life is life. The solution is not other people. It is yourself. Your salvation lies within your own soul. The future belongs to those who prepare for it today.

We seek to glorify our existence when our existence is our only glory.

Dance beneath the indifferent stars. Be grateful for every day you wake up and live.

You would think that given our knowledge of the physics, chemistry and biology of the universe, that everyone would be grateful to just be alive, given that it is a miracle that we are in fact alive. But sadly, we are not. Very few people are aware that the universe exists. That is how powerful the illusion of life is. In contrast most are consumed by the system that meaning becomes marriage and work. But that is only a fabricated or cosmetic meaning. The true reality is that life is purposeless.

The Path
'There is no right or wrong path.'

There are an infinite number of paths by which one can live life. The saddest part of life is that we dare not question it. We casually accept the path laid out for us without even the faintest reprimand. The question is not who or what will change your life, but what will you do to change your life.

There is a schism in the soul of man. A battle rages between the demands of conformity and the yearning to go his own path.

And no one byway takes precedent over another.

Nobody can give you freedom. Nobody can give you life. You have to earn it. You have to take it. You have to walk down that path by yourself. The world will not provide.

Conformity is a worn-out path and one will never achieve much in life by following the same course that everyone else follows.

At best most people achieve only mediocrity. This is the common goal, the common deceit.

We see how others live their lives and we instinctively follow them without hesitation.

We are most blind when we most engage with life. The secret to a good life is in realizing you are alive.

Far too many people escape into life itself as a means to forget the realities of this universe. People thus conform willingly.

They firmly believe in their emotion that marriage and work is the only means to live. It becomes the only avenue.

They are so doped on this that the path of individuality is passed by. You die in mediocrity because the most you aim for is mediocrity.

People don't realize what they do. They know what they want out of life but are puzzled to why they want it.

The instinctive drive to conform clouds their reason. They live on spontaneous decision and see only one route in life.

Conformity is a path to live but not the only path by which one lives.

There are so many ways to live our lives and yet we converge towards one solitary goal.

And you will not achieve much by living as everyone else lives.

Man must find his own path and his own meaning to live. Do not conform for its own sake.

A naïve man says: When I achieve so much I will be happy. A smart man says: I am happy so much because I can achieve so much.

One achieves far more by being who they are rather than letting others choose who they are. Life is the ultimate paradox. The more you try to live the less you do. The more you try to find meaning the more time you waste in not living.

If you can be taught to want in life; you can be taught to just be happy. One must simply train their unconscious.

The greatest courage is in being who you are in spite of the world wanting you to be someone else. Individuality is the sunrise and sunset of existence.

Do not venture on the rocky roads of life to succeed. Venture on them to be yourself, to enjoy them and you will succeed. The goal of existence is to love it.

The only path is your path and the curiosity of going your own way. The ability of man to choose his own path and his own salvation is his genius.

A man to truly value his life would have to die a hundred times. Why do we live if we face a certain death? If your motivations are anything except to love life and love your existence, you are wasting your time. Your only motivation, the only motivation needed is to love your existence.

The universe is perpetual darkness and indifference and no matter how bleary we must radiate our own light. There is no rainbow without the rain. Existence is your substance; the ability to choose your own path is your genius.

The only thing I can say with certainty is that a life, no matter how cruel, how despairing and how indifferent, is better than no life at all.

Final Word: Gratitude vs Gratification

'Be grateful for your existence.'

I too was once polluted by the disease of capitalism. I would admonish myself for not being of the appropriate standard. I would internally castigate my soul for failing to meet the requirements of the capitalist ideology. It was only when I found myself silhouetted against a vast vibrant yet indifferent universe that I finally became one with my existence. The problem was that I was schooled on the two-dimensional aspects of life: Work and Relationships and as such my daily life was centred around them. I knew of no other way in which to live. It was only in the deep quietness of solitude that I discovered myself. From my own experience my existential freedom enables me to live alone without feeling guilty. Before I would lament my weakness. I didn't have a relationship or I wasn't working in the ideal job and I would berate myself for my failures. By becoming existentially free I was no longer engrossed in this shallow race. I began to gain enjoyment from the simpler things in life such as just being alive. I was no longer judging myself against others. I was no longer envious of others. My life is much simpler now and I am much happier for it. Become free in the despairing moonlight. You are lucky to exist in this universe. Forget about your life as you know it. Don't think of your friends or your career. Think about the majestic darkness that encompasses your existence and find your consolation within it. In this universe your fortune is not money, not love and not success but rather existence. Existence is your genius.

We are condemned to chase in life. We cannot sit and tolerate our own being. We pursue enjoyment. This is a consequence of language. Gratification is an addictive happiness. It is one in which the individual must obtain in life to be content. It is poison. Gratitude is the most sublime happiness of all. Gratitude is when you appreciate the journey because you realize how fortunate you are to be alive and to be able to journey through life. The only gratification of worth is gratitude. Gratification is existing to enjoy; gratitude is enjoying your existence. The world is your glory. That you are alive and able to see and hear and sense this magnificent stage is all the happiness you need. Do not waste your life in search of a better one, for the one you have is plentiful. Find nourishment in the sunrise and sunset and every second in between. Be in love with every synapse of your calling.

Nietzsche once said that the individual must struggle to overcome the current of conformity. This wind of desire is strong and forceful and many men wilt to its power. The herd extols conformism at all costs and men can only but bow to what is requested of them. We are like soldiers at war who run head first into the enemy fire all because we were ordered to do so. How many of those frightened men have the courage to disavow the general's commands? Becoming your own individual is what a man should aspire to in life. To live by your own conscience and not the hand of conventionalism is freedom. "But no price is too high," he said "to pay for the privilege of owning oneself." This is what existential therapy sets out to do: To make man summon his own life instead of succumbing to the stream of conventionalism. Life is rudderless and we float with the tide of popular opinion. We all die freely so one may as well live freely.

The one thing I wish people to take from my notes is this: If you have read these notes it means you exist and if you exist be eternally grateful for existing. Just be happy to be alive. Your success in life is being able to wake up every day. Be happy to be alive.

If you enjoyed this book, I recommend that you purchase the follow up "Remarks On Existential Nihilism: Labelling, Narcissism and Existential Maturity."